ECONOMIC ISSUES, PROBLEMS AND PERSPECTIVES

ESTATE AND GIFT TAXES: ECONOMICS AND HISTORY

Economic Issues, Problems and Perspectives

Additional books in this series can be found on Nova's website under the Series tab.

Additional E-books in this series can be found on Nova's website under the E-books tab.

ECONOMIC ISSUES, PROBLEMS AND PERSPECTIVES

ESTATE AND GIFT TAXES: ECONOMICS AND HISTORY

Jacob A. Hughes
EDITOR

Nova Science Publishers, Inc.
New York

For permission to use material from this book please contact us:
Telephone 631-231-7269; Fax 631-231-8175
Web Site: http://www.novapublishers.com

Library of Congress Cataloging-in-Publication Data

Estate and gift taxes : economics and history / editor, Jacob A. Hughes.
p. cm.
Includes index.
"CRS report for Congress prepared for members and committees of Congress."
ISBN 978-1-62100-516-2 (hardcover)
1. Inheritance and transfer tax--United States. I. Gravelle, Jane. II. Maguire, Steven.
KF6571.A25 2011
336.2'760973--dc23

2011035483

Published by Nova Science Publishers, Inc. ✝ New York

CONTENTS

PREFACE

The United States tax system includes a tax on assets held at death, the estate tax and the gift tax. Among key components of the estate and gift tax are the definition of its taxable base, tax rate and exemption level. A related argument is that the tax reduces the concentration of wealth and its perceived adverse consequences for society. Critics of the estate and gift tax make two major arguments: the estate and gift tax discourages savings and investments, and the tax imposes an undue burden on closely held family businesses. Critics also suggest that the estate and gift tax is flawed as a method of introducing progressivity because there are many methods of avoiding the tax, methods that are more available to very wealthy families. This book provides an explanation of how the tax operates, analyzes the arguments for and against the tax and discusses alternative policy options.

Chapter 1- The United State tax system includes a tax on assets held at death, the estate tax, and on wealth transfers made while living, the gift tax. Among the key components of the estate and gift tax are the definition of its taxable base, tax rate, and exemption level. Historically, the latter two components have been administratively linked. The Economic Growth and Tax Relief Reconciliation Act of 2001 (EGTRRA) dramatically changed several aspects of the federal estate and gift tax, by gradually reducing the maximum tax rate and the raising the effective estate and gift tax exemption until repealing the estate tax in 2010. In 2010 the federal gift tax would remain, though the rate would be reduced to the top personal income tax rate and with an exemption separate from the estate tax exemption. After repeal of the estate tax, carryover basis replaces step-up in basis for assets transferred at death. The act included an exemption from carryover basis for capital gains of $1.3 million (and an additional $3 million for a surviving spouse). However, the estate tax provision in EGTRRA automatically sunsets December 31, 2010.

Chapter 2- The Economic Growth and Tax Relief Reconciliation Act of 2001 (EGTRRA; P.L. 107-16), among other tax cuts, provided for a gradual reduction and elimination of the estate tax. Under EGTRRA, the estate tax exemption rose from $675,000 in 2001 to $3.5 million in 2009, and the rate fell from 55% to 45%. In 2010, the estate tax was eliminated. As with other provisions, however, the estate tax changes were scheduled to sunset in 2011 when the exemption would have become $1 million (as scheduled in pre-EGTRRA law) and the tax rate would return to 55.

Chapter 3- In 2010, the first year since 1916, there was no federal estate tax. There was also a year hiatus for the generation-skipping tax. The Economic Growth and Tax Relief Reconciliation Act of 2001 (P.L. 107-16) provided for a phaseout of the estate and generation-skipping taxes over a 10-year period, leaving the gift tax as the only federal transfer tax in 2010. The Tax Relief, Unemployment Insurance Reauthorization, and Job Creation Act of 2010 (P.L. 111-312) marked, at least, the suspension, if not the termination, of the movement away from the transfer taxes. The act temporarily (through the end of 2012) reinstated the estate and generation-skipping taxes with lower top rates (35%) and larger exemptions ($5,000,000) and reunified the estate and gift taxes. The act was effective on January 1, 2011, but estates of decendents dying in 2010 were given the option of electing coverage by the reinsted estate tax or keeping the carry-over basis for inherited assets.

Chapter 4- This report contains an explanation of the major provisions of the federal estate, gift, and generation-skipping transfer taxes as they apply to transfers in 2011. The discussion provides basic principles to be applied in the computation of these three transfer taxes.

The federal estate and generation-skipping taxes were resurrected by the Tax Relief, Unemployment Insurance Reauthorization, and Job Creation Act of 2010 (P.L. 111-312) after a hiatus of one year (2010). This act also provided elective options for estates of those who died in 2010.

Chapter 5- This report provides data on the distribution of assets in estates as reported on estate tax returns filed in 2009. This report finds that farm and business assets represent a small share of the total value of taxable estates that filed tax returns in 2009, (3.25% and 13.86%, respectively). That share is concentrated in estates valued over $10 million.

Chapter 6- The 2001 tax revision began a phaseout of the estate tax, by increasing exemptions and lowering rates. The estate tax is scheduled to be repealed in 2010 and a provision to tax appreciation on inherited assets (in excess of a limit) will be substituted. The 2001 tax provisions sunset, however, so that absent a change making them permanent the estate tax will revert, in 2011, to prior, pre-2001 law. Proposals to make the repeal permanent, or to significantly increase the exemptions and lower the rate, are under consideration.

Chapter 7- P.L. 107-16, the Economic Growth and Tax Relief Reconciliation Act of 2001, repeals the federal estate tax for 2010 decedents. In addition, the act repealed the credit for state estate taxes for individuals dying after December 31, 2004, and replaced the credit with a deduction. In most states, the repeal of the tax and the significant increase in the federal exclusion will also repeal or diminish state estate, inheritance, and gift taxes. Some state budgets depend on the estate tax more than others. As a percentage of total tax revenue collected from FY2001 to FY2004, state estate tax contributions ranged from 0.19% in Alaska to 3.15% in Pennsylvania. After the federal credit for state estate taxes changed to a deduction in 2005, revenue collected from this tax source declined significantly, and in 2010, 29 states no longer levied estate or inheritance taxes. In the 111th Congress, H.R. 4154, passed by the House of Representatives on December 3, 2009, would permanently set the estate tax exemption level at $3.5 million per decedent, and proposals currently under consideration in the Senate would similarly retain the estate tax after repeal in 2010.

In: Estate and Gift Taxes
Editor: Jacob A. Hughes

ISBN: 978-1-62100-516-2

Chapter 1

ESTATE AND GIFT TAXES: ECONOMIC ISSUES*

Donald J. Marples and Jane G. Gravelle

SUMMARY

The United State tax system includes a tax on assets held at death, the estate tax, and on wealth transfers made while living, the gift tax. Among the key components of the estate and gift tax are the definition of its taxable base, tax rate, and exemption level. Historically, the latter two components have been administratively linked. The Economic Growth and Tax Relief Reconciliation Act of 2001 (EGTRRA) dramatically changed several aspects of the federal estate and gift tax, by gradually reducing the maximum tax rate and the raising the effective estate and gift tax exemption until repealing the estate tax in 2010. In 2010 the federal gift tax would remain, though the rate would be reduced to the top personal income tax rate and with an exemption separate from the estate tax exemption. After repeal of the estate tax, carryover basis replaces step-up in basis for assets transferred at death. The act included an exemption from carryover basis for capital gains of $1.3 million (and an additional $3 million for a surviving spouse). However, the estate tax provision in EGTRRA automatically sunsets December 31, 2010.

* This is an edited, reformatted and augmented version of a Congressional Research Service publication, CRS Report for Congress RL30600, from www.crs.gov, dated December 4, 2009.

Amid concerns about the lack of certainty and other issues, including the administrative challenges of carryover basis, several proposals have been discussed to address these changes in the estate tax. One proposal would extend the 2009 rules, which provide a $3.5 million exemption and a 45% tax rate, through 2010. President Obama's budget proposed making rules applicable for 2009, with a $3.5 million exemption and a 45% tax rate, permanent. Legislation, most recently H.R. 4154 (which passed in the House on December 3, 2009), would make these provisions permanent. The Joint Committee on Taxation has estimated the cost through 2019 to be $234 billion. Other legislation would permanently repeal the estate tax or retain the tax but increase the exemption and/or lower the rate. Legislation has also been proposed to address certain avoidance techniques, such as preventing the lowering of valuation by the courts through family partnerships.

Supporters of the estate and gift tax cite its contribution to progressivity in the tax system and to the need for a tax due to the forgiveness of capital gains taxes on appreciated assets held until death. Arguments are also made that inheritances represent a windfall to heirs that are more appropriate sources of tax revenue than income earned through work and effort. Critics of the estate tax argue that it reduces savings and makes it difficult to pass on family businesses. Critics also argue that death is not an appropriate time to impose a tax; that much wealth has already been taxed through income taxes; and that complexity of the tax imposes administrative and compliance burdens that undermine the progressivity of the tax.

The analysis in this study suggests that the estate tax is highly progressive, although progressivity is undermined by avoidance mechanisms. Neither economic theory nor empirical evidence indicate that the estate tax is likely to have much effect on savings. Although some family businesses are burdened by the tax, only a small percentage of estate tax revenues are derived from family businesses. Even though there are many estate tax avoidance techniques, it also is possible to reform the tax and reduce these complexities as an alternative to eliminating the tax. Thus, the evaluation of the estate tax may largely turn on the appropriateness of such a revenue source and its interaction with incentives for charitable giving, state estate taxes, and capital gains and other income taxes.

INTRODUCTION

The United State tax system includes a tax on assets held at death, the estate tax, and on wealth transfers made while living, the gift tax. Among the key components of the estate and gift tax are the definition of its taxable base, tax rate, and exemption level.

The estate and gift tax has been and will continue to be the subject of significant legislative interest. The "Economic Growth and Tax Relief Reconciliation Act of 2001" (EGTRRA, P.L. 107-16) repealed the estate tax after 2009. However, the legislation sunsets after 2010 reverting back to the law as it existed in 2001. Congress could eliminate the sunset provision in EGTRRA, thus making repeal of the estate tax permanent. Repeal of the sunset would retain the EGTRRA changes to the taxation of capital gains of inherited assets and the gift tax.

Immediate repeal of the estate and gift tax in 2001 would have cost up to $662 billion (over 10 years), an amount in excess of the projected estate tax yield of $409 billion because of projected behavioral responses that would also lower income tax revenues (e.g., more life time transfers to donees in lower tax brackets, more purchase of life insurance with deferral aspects, and lower compliance). Repealing the EGTRRA sunset would cost $522 billion over the 2009-2018 budget window. Most of the revenue loss would be in the "out" years; $149.7 billion over 2009 to 2013 and $372.3 billion over 2014 to 2018.[1] Immediate repeal (as opposed to eventual repeal beyond 2010) would be more expensive.

Amid concerns about the lack of certainty and other issues, including the administrative challenges of the carryover basis, several proposals have been discussed to address these changes in the estate tax. One proposal would extend the 2009 rules, which provide a $3.5 million exemption and a 45% tax rate, through 2010. President Obama's budget proposed making rules applicable for 2009, with a $3.5 million exemption and a 45% tax rate, permanent. Legislation, most recently H.R. 4154 (which passed the House on December 3, 2009), would make these provisions permanent. The Joint Committee on Taxation has estimated H.R. 4154 to cost $234 billion through 2019; the Treasury has estimated the President's proposal at $171 billion.[2] Other legislation would permanently repeal the estate tax or retain the tax but increase the exemption and/or lower the rate. Legislation has also been proposed to address certain avoidance techniques, such as preventing the lowering of valuation by the courts through family partnerships.

Proponents of an estate and gift tax argue that it contributes to progressivity in the tax system by "taxing the rich." (Note, however, that there is no way to objectively determine the optimal degree of progressivity in a tax system.) A related argument is that the tax reduces the concentration of wealth and its perceived adverse consequences for society.[3] Moreover, while the estate and gift tax is relatively small as a revenue source (yielding $26 billion in 2007 and accounting for 1% of federal revenue), it raises a not insignificant amount of revenue—revenue that could increase in the future in the event of strong performance of stock market and growth in inter-generational transfers as the baby boom generation ages. Eliminating or reducing the tax would either require some other tax to be increased, some spending program to be reduced, or an increase in the national debt.

In addition, to the extent that inherited wealth is seen as windfall to the recipient, such a tax may be seen by some as fairer than taxing earnings that are the result of work and effort. Finally, many economists suggest that an important rationale for maintaining an estate tax is the escape of unrealized capital gains from any taxation, since heirs receive a stepped-up basis of assets. Families that accrue large gains through the appreciation of their wealth in assets can, in the absence of an estate tax, largely escape any taxes on these gains by passing on the assets to their heirs.

The estate tax also encourages giving to charity, since charitable contributions are deductible from the estate tax base. Since charitable giving is generally recognized as an appropriate object of subsidy, the presence of an estate tax with such a deduction may be seen as one of the potential tools for encouraging charitable giving.

Critics of the estate and gift tax typically make two major arguments: the estate and gift tax discourages savings and investments, and the tax imposes an undue burden on closely held family businesses (including farms). In the latter case, the argument is made that the estate tax forces the break-up of family businesses without adequate liquidity to pay the tax. Critics also suggest that the estate and gift tax is flawed as a method of introducing progressivity because there are many methods of avoiding the tax, methods that are more available to very wealthy families (although this criticism could support reform of the tax as well as repeal). A related criticism is that the administrative and compliance cost of an estate and gift tax is onerous relative to its yield (again, however, this argument could also be advanced to support reform rather than repeal). In general, there may also be a feeling that death is not a desirable time to impose a tax; indeed, the critics of the estate and gift tax often refer to the tax as a death tax. Critics also argue that some of the wealth passed on in estates has generally already been subject to capital income taxes.

The remainder of this report, following a brief explanation of how the tax operates, analyzes these arguments for and against the tax. The report concludes with an inventory and discussion of alternative policy options.

How the Estate and Gift Tax Works

The unified estate and gift tax is levied on the transfer of assets that occurs when someone dies or gives a gift. Filing an estate tax return can be difficult depending on the value and complexity of the estate. The purpose here is to outline the mechanics of the estate and gift tax. The first section begins with a brief review of the general rules accompanied with a numerical example. There are some minor provisions of the law that are not discussed here, however, such as the phase out of the graduated rates and the credit for taxes on property recently transferred.[4] The second section summarizes the special rules for farms and small businesses. And, the final section briefly describes the generation skipping transfer tax. The Appendix of this report provides detailed data from returns filed in 2007, the latest year for which data are available.

General Rules

Filing Threshold

In 2009, estates valued over $3.5 million must file an estate tax return. The applicable credit, which is identical to the filing threshold, effectively exempts from taxation the portion of the estate that falls below the filing threshold. (The filing threshold is lower, however, if gifts have already been made.) Table A-1 in the Appendix reports the current filing requirement and the unified credit equivalent for 2004 through 2011.

Gross Estate Value

The gross estate value, which was $203 billion for returns filed in 2007, is the total value of all property and assets owned by decedents. Table A-2 in the Appendix provides the gross estate value for returns filed in 2007 by wealth category. The data represent the returns filed in 2007, not the decedents in that year. Thus, a portion of the returns filed in 2007 are from estates valued in years before 2007.

Allowable Deductions

Deductions from the estate reduce the taxable portion of the gross estate and in turn the number of taxable returns. In 2007, $93.2 billion was deducted from estates. The most valuable deduction is for bequests to a surviving spouse, $62 billion; the most prevalent (though smallest reported) deduction is for funeral expenses, $340.6 million. Table A-3 lists the deductions in greater detail for returns filed in 2007. Beginning in 2005, estates may deduct state estate taxes paid. Before 2005, taxpayers received a federal credit for state death taxes paid. That credit was phased out incrementally from 2002 through 2004.

Taxable Estate

After subtracting allowable deductions, the remainder of the estate is the taxable estate. Taxable estate value was $112.1 billion in 2007. Adjusted taxable gifts are then added to the taxable estate to arrive upon the adjusted taxable estate. An individual is allowed to exclude $12,000 in gifts per year per donee from taxable gifts. Thus, only the amount exceeding the $12,000 limit is added back to the taxable estate. Only 8,384 returns filed in 2007 included taxable gifts, adding approximately $8.3 billion to the total estate value. Thus, adjusted taxable estates were worth $120.5 billion in 2007. Generally, the adjusted taxable estate represents the base of estate tax.

Rates and Brackets

After establishing the value of the taxable estate, the executor calculates the tentative estate tax due.[5] The tax due is tentative because the executor has not redeemed the applicable credit amount.[6] As noted earlier, the credit for state estate and inheritance taxes was repealed and replaced with a deduction beginning in 2005.

A Numerical Example

The remaining steps in calculating the estate and gift tax are most easily exhibited through numerical example. To accomplish this, we first assume a decedent, who dies in 2009, has an estate worth $10 million and leaves $2 million to his wife and contributes $400,000 to a charitable organization. We also assume the decedent has not made any taxable gifts leaving $2.6 million in his estate after deductions. This simple example is exhibited below.

The taxable estate is valued at $2.6 million after the allowable deductions have been subtracted from the gross estate value.[7] The tax is applied to the $2.6 million in increments of estate value as provided for in the tax code. For example, the first increment of $10,000 is taxed at 18%, the second increment of $10,000 is taxed at 20%, the third increment of $20,000 is taxed at 22%, etc. This process continues until the entire $2.6 million is taxed. The last increment of estate value, that from $1.5 million to $2.6 million, is taxed at a

45% rate. Thus, even though this estate is in the 45% bracket, only a portion ($1.1 million) of the estate is taxed at the 45% rate.

Table 1. Numerical Example (applying 2008 rules)

Gross Estate Value	$5,000,000
—Less: hypothetical marital deduction	$2,000,000
—Less: hypothetical charitable contribution deduction	$400,000
Taxable Estate	**$2,600,000**

Tentative Estate Tax

In 2007, the aggregate tentative estate tax after deductions and before credits was $46.4 billion. Returning to our example, the $2.6 million taxable estate yields a tentative estate tax of $1,050,800. Recall, however, we have not yet considered the "applicable credit."

The Applicable Credit (Unified with Gift Tax before 2004)

For decedents dying in 2009, the applicable credit is $780,800, which leaves an estate tax due in our example of $270,000. The applicable credit reduced the national aggregate tentative estate tax by $27.4 billion in 2007.

Federal Credit for State Death Taxes (Eliminated in 2005)

The state death tax credit reduced the federal estate tax due by $261.5 million in 2006.[8] This tax credit is determined by yet another tax rate schedule. The taxable estate value, which is $2.6 million in our example, is reduced by a standard exemption of $60,000 and the credit rate schedule applies to the remainder. EGTRRA reduces and eventually repeals the credit for state death taxes. In 2004, the credit was 25% of what the credit would have been before EGTRRA. In 2005, the credit was repealed and estates were allowed to deduct state death taxes paid. Table A-5 of the Appendix reproduces the now-repealed credit schedule for state death taxes. For our hypothetical estate filed in 2008 the credit is not available and thus state death taxes would be deductible. In many states, however, the state estate tax is repealed along with the federal credit.

Net Federal Estate Tax

The net estate tax due was $22.5 billion in 2007.[9] This is the final step for the estate executor. After all exemptions, deductions, and credits, the $5 million dollar estate we began with must now remit $270,000 to the federal government.

All of the steps described above are included in Table 2. Also, an estimate of the average estate tax rate is presented in the bottom row. The federal rate is calculated as the federal estate tax due divided by the gross estate value.

Table 2. Numerical Example Continued with Taxes and Credits (applying 2008 rules)

Gross Estate Value	$5,000,000
—Less: hypothetical marital deduction	$2,000,000
—Less: hypothetical charitable contribution deduction	$400,000
Taxable Estate	**$2,600,000**
Tentative Estate Tax (from the rate schedule)	$1,050,800
—Less: Applicable Credit Amount (in 2008)	$780,800
Net Federal Estate Tax	**$270,000**
Average Effective Federal Estate Tax Rate	**5.40%**

SPECIAL RULES FOR FAMILY OWNED FARMS AND BUSINESSES

There are primarily two special rules for family owned farms and businesses. The first special rule (26 I.R.C. 6166) allows family owned farm and business estates to pay the tax in installments over a maximum of 10 years after a deferment of up to five years. The farm or business must comprise at least 35% of the adjusted gross estate value to qualify for the installment method. A portion of the deferred estate tax is assessed an annual 2% interest charge.

The second special rule (26 I.R.C. 2032A) allows family farms and businesses that meet certain requirements to value their land as currently used rather than at fair market value. To avoid a recapture tax, heirs must continue to use the land as designated in the special use notice for at least 10 years following the transfer. The market value could be reduced by a maximum $750,000 in 1998. After 1998, the maximum is indexed for inflation, rounded to the next lowest multiple of $10,000. In 2008, the maximum was $960,000.

The Generation Skipping Transfer Tax

Generally, the generation skipping transfer (GST) tax is levied on transfers from the decedent to grandchildren. The tax includes a $2,000,000 exemption per donor in 2008 that is pegged to the general estate tax exclusion. Married couples are allowed to "split" their gifts for an effective exemption of $3,000,000. The rate of tax is the highest estate and gift tax rate or 45% in 2008 These transfers are also subject to applicable estate and gift taxes. The GST exemption rises to $3.5 million in 2009. Very few estates pay a generation skipping transfer tax because the high rate of tax discourages this type of bequest.

ECONOMIC ISSUES

As noted in the "Introduction," the principal arguments surrounding the estate and gift tax are associated with the desirability of reducing the concentration of wealth and income through the tax and the possible adverse effect of the tax on savings behavior and family businesses. There are a number of other issues of fairness or efficiency associated with particular aspects of the tax (e.g., marital deductions, charitable deductions, effects on small businesses, interaction with capital gains taxes) , and the possible contribution to tax complexity. These issues are addressed in this section.

The Distributional Effect of the Estate and Gift Tax

Distributional effects concern both vertical equity (how high income individuals are affected relative to low income individuals) and horizontal equity (how individuals in equal circumstances are differentially affected). Note that economic analysis cannot be used to determine the optimal degree of distribution across income and wealth (vertical equity).

Vertical Equity

The estate tax is the most progressive of any of the federal taxes; out of the approximately 2.4 million deaths in 2005, only 0.8% of estates paid any estate tax.[10] This percentage can be contrasted with the income tax where most families and single individuals file tax returns and about 70% of those returns owe tax. In addition, out of the 0.8% of decedents whose estates pay tax, about 50% of these had gross estates valued between $1.5 million and $3.5 million in 2005, which are the smallest (based on gross estate value) taxable estates.

Evidence suggests that the average effective tax rate rises with the size of the estate except for the highest tax rate bracket, as shown in Table 3 [columns (f) and (g)]. Column (f) reports 2007 effective tax rates for the decedent before the credit for state death taxes and column (g) shows the actual amount paid to the federal government after all credits. Estates valued at less than the exemption amount, of course, pay no taxes and the tax rate rises and then falls with the very largest estates, despite the fact that the rates are graduated.

Columns (b), (c), and (d) show the deductions from the estate as a percentage of gross estate value. Charitable deductions are the primary reason for the lower tax rate in the highest levels of the estate tax. The charitable deduction accounts for 9.7% of estates on average but 21.24% in the highest wealth bracket. The deduction for bequests left to spouse also rises as a portion of the gross estate as estate size increases. The progressivity of the estate tax for the estates valued at less than $10 million is the result of the unified credit and the graduated rate structure.

The data in Table 3 may actually overstate the amount of rate progression in the estate tax. Tax planning techniques, such as gift tax exclusions or valuation discounts, reduce the size of the gross estate and are more common with larger estates. These techniques reduce the size of the estate but do not appear in the IRS data, thus, the effective tax rates may be overstated for larger estates.

Despite the lack of progressivity through all of the estate size brackets, the principal point for distributional purposes is that the estate and gift tax is confined to the wealthiest of decedents and to a tiny share of the population. For example, estates over $5 million accounted for 26.7% of taxable estates, but accounted for 78.4% of estate tax revenues in 2007. Thus, to the extent that concentration of income and wealth are viewed as undesirable, the estate tax plays some role, albeit small—because few pay the tax—in increasing income and wealth equality.

Note also an effect that contradicts some claims made by opponents of the tax. The Carnegie conjecture suggests that large inheritances reduce labor effort by heirs.[11] Thus, the estate tax, which reduces inheritances, could increase output and economic growth because heirs work more (increase their labor supply) if their inheritance is reduced. Although, for very large inheritances, the effect of one individual on the labor supply may be small relative to the effect on saving.

Table 3. Estate Tax Deductions and Burdens, 2007

Size of Gross Estate ($ millions)	Percent of Gross Estate			Tax as a Percent of Net Estatea		
	Expenses	Bequests to Spouse	Charity	Before Credit	After Unified Credit	After All Creditsb
(a)	(b)	(c)	(d)	(e)	(f)	(g)
2.0-3.5	5.07%	19.14%	3.85%	30.39%	0.47%	4.81%
3.5-5.0	5.31%	28.20%	4.85%	27.48%	8.72%	10.23%
5.0-10.0	5.98%	32.58%	6.02%	26.49%	14.82%	14.96%
10.0-20.0	5.67%	37.17%	6.53%	25.12%	19.34%	18.36%
over 20.0	5.78%	38.92%	21.24%	16.99%	15.64%	14.60%
Total	5.56%	30.56%	9.70%	24.96%	10.69%	11.74%

Source: CRS calculations from Statistics of Income, *Estate Tax Returns Filed in 2007*, IRS, SOI unpublished data, October 2008.

[a] Net estate is estate value less expenses. Expenses include funeral expenses, attorney's fees, executors' commissions, other expenses/losses, and debts and mortgages.

[b] This includes any gift taxes that are owed by an estate, which could increase the total taxes owed by an estate.

Horizontal Equity

Estate and gift taxes can affect similar individuals differentially for a variety of reasons. Special provisions for farmers and family businesses (discussed subsequently) can cause families with the same amount of wealth to be taxed differentially. The availability and differential use of avoidance techniques (also discussed subsequently) can lead to different tax burdens for the same amount of wealth. Moreover, individuals who accumulate similar amounts of wealth may pay differential taxes depending on how long they live.

Effect on Saving

Many people presume that the estate tax reduces savings, since the estate and gift tax, like a capital income tax, applies to wealth. It may appear "obvious" that a tax on wealth would reduce wealth. However, taxes on capital income do not necessarily reduce savings. This ambiguous result arises from the opposing forces of an income and substitution effect. An investment is made to provide future consumption; if the rate of return rises because a tax is cut, more consumption might be shifted from the present to the future (the substitution effect). This effect, in isolation, would increase saving.

However, the tax savings also increases the return earned on investment and allows higher consumption both today and in the future. This effect is called an income effect, and it tends to reduce saving. Its effect is most pronounced when the savings is for a fixed target (such as a fund for college tuition or a target bequest to an heir). Thus, saving for precautionary reasons (as a hedge against bad events) is less likely to increase when the rate of return rises than saving for retirement. Empirical evidence on savings responses, while difficult to obtain, suggests a small effect of uncertain sign (i.e., either positive or negative). Current events certainly suggest that savings fall when the rate of return rises: as returns on stocks have increased dramatically, the savings rate has plunged.

The same points can generally be made about a tax on estates and gifts, although some analysts suspect that an estate tax, to be paid at a distant date in the future, would be less likely to have an effect (in either direction) than income taxes being paid currently. A reduction in estate taxes makes a larger net bequest possible, reducing the price of the bequest in terms of forgone consumption. This substitution effect would cause savings to increase. At the same time, a reduction in estate taxes causes the net estate to be larger, allowing a larger net bequest to be made with a smaller amount of savings (the income effect). Again, the latter effect is most pronounced when there is a target net bequest; a smaller gross bequest can be left (and less savings required on the part of the decedent) to achieve the net target.

Unfortunately, virtually no empirical evidence about the effect of estate and gift taxes exists, in part because these taxes have been viewed as small and relatively unimportant by most researchers and in part because there are tremendous difficulties in trying to link an estate and gift tax which occurs at the end of a lifetime to annual savings behavior. But a reasonable expectation is that the effects of cutting the estate and gift tax on savings would not be large and would not even necessarily be positive.

Of course, the effect on national saving depends on the use to which tax revenues are put. If revenues are used to decrease the national debt, they become part of government saving, and it is more likely that cutting estate and gift taxes would reduce saving by decreasing government saving, since there may be little or no effect on private saving. If they are used for government spending on consumption programs, or transfers that are primarily used for consumption, then it is less likely that cutting estate and gift taxes would reduce saving because the estate tax cut would be financed out of decreased consumption (rather than decreased saving). In this case, reducing the tax would probably have a small effect on national saving, since the evidence suggests a small effect on private saving. A similar effect would occur if tax revenues are held constant and the alternative tax primarily reduced consumption.

Actually, the estate and gift tax is, in some ways, more complicated to assess than a tax on capital income or wealth. There are a variety of possible motives for leaving bequests, which are likely to cause savings to respond differently to the estate tax. In addition, there are consequences for the heirs which may affect their savings.

Several of these alternative motives and their consequences are outlined by Gale and Perozek.[12] Motives for leaving bequests include (1) altruism: individuals want to increase the welfare of their children and other descendants because they care about them; (2) accident: individuals do not intentionally save to leave a bequest but as a fund to cover unexpected costs or the costs of living longer than expected (thus, bequests are left by accident and are in the nature of precautionary savings); (3) exchange: parents promise to leave bequests to their children in exchange for services (visiting, looking after parents when they are sick); and (4) joy of giving: individuals get pleasure directly from giving, with the pleasure depending on the size of the estate. To Gale and Perozek's classifications we might add satiation: when individuals have so much wealth that any consumption desire can be met.

The theoretical effects of these alternative theories on decedents and heirs are summarized in Table 4. A discussion of each follows in the text, but it is interesting to see that there is a tendency for estate taxes to increase saving, not decrease it. This effect occurs in part because there are "double" income effects that discourage consumption, acting on both the decedent and the heir.

Altruistic

When giving is motivated by altruism, the effect of the tax is ambiguous, as might not be surprising given the discussion of income and substitution effects. The effects on the parents are ambiguous, while the windfall receipt of an inheritance tends to reduce the need to save by the children. That is, the estate tax reduces the inheritances and thus increases saving by heirs. The outcomes are also partly dependent on whether children think they can elicit a larger inheritance by squandering their own money (which causes them to save even less) and whether the parent sees this problem and responds to it in a way that forestalls it. Interestingly, some parents might respond by spending a lot of their assets before death to induce their children to be more responsible and save more. The cost of doing this is the reduction in welfare of their children from the smaller bequest as compared with the parent's benefit from consumption. The estate tax actually makes the cost of using this method smaller (in terms of reduced bequests for each dollar spent), and causes the parents to consume more. While these motivations and actions of parent and child can become complex, this theory leaves us with an ambiguous effect on savings.

Accidental

In the second case, where bequests are left because parents die before they have exhausted their resources, the estate tax has no effect on the saving of the parents. Indeed, the parents are not really concerned about the estate tax since it has no effect on the reason they are accumulating assets. If they need the assets because they live too long or become ill, no tax will be paid. Bequests are a windfall to children, in this case, and tend to increase their consumption. Thus, taxing bequests, because it reduces this windfall, reduces their consumption and promotes savings. If the revenue from the estate tax is saved by the government, national saving rises. (If the revenue is spent on consumption, there is no effect on savings.) Thus, in this case, the estate tax reduces private consumption and repealing it, reducing the surplus, would increase consumption (reduce savings).

Exchange

In the third case, parents are basically paying for children's services with bequests and the estate tax becomes like a tax on products: the price for their children's attention has increased. Not surprisingly, the savings and size of bequest by the parents depends on how responsive they are to these price changes. If the demand is less responsive to price changes (price inelastic), parents will save and bequeath more to make up for the tax to be sure of receiving their children's services, but if there are close substitutes they might save less, bequeath less, and purchase alternatives (e.g., nursing home care). In this model, the child's saving is not affected, since the bequest is payment for forgone wages (or leisure).

Table 4. Theoretical Effect of Estate Tax on Saving, By Bequest Motive

Bequest Motive	Effect on Decedent Saving	Effect on Heir Saving
Altruism	Ambiguous	Increases
Accidental	None	Increases
Exchange	Ambiguous	None
Joy of Giving	Ambiguous	Increases
Satiation	None	Increases or None

Joy of Giving

A fourth motive is called the "joy-of-giving" motive, where individuals simply enjoy leaving a bequest. If the parent focuses on the before-tax bequest, the estate tax will have no effect on his or her behavior, but will reduce the inheritance and theoretically increase the saving of children. Thus, repealing the estate tax would reduce private saving. If the parent focuses on the after-tax bequest, the effect on saving is ambiguous (again, due to income and substitution effects).

Satiation

Some families may be so wealthy that they can satisfy all of their consumption needs without feeling any constraints and their wealth accumulation may be a (large) residual. In this case, as well, the estate tax would have no effect on saving of the donor, and perhaps little effect on the donee as well.

Empirical Evidence

Evidence for these motives is not clear but this analysis does suggest that there are many circumstances in which a repeal of the estate tax would reduce savings, not increase it. Virtually no work has been done to estimate the effect of estate taxes on accumulation of assets. A preliminary analysis of estate tax data by Kopczuk and Slemrod found some limited evidence of a negative effect on savings, but this effect was not robust (i.e., did not persist with changes in data sets or specification).[13] This effect was relatively small in any case and the authors stress the many limitations of their results. In particular, their analysis cannot distinguish between the reduction of estates due to savings responses and those due to tax avoidance techniques.

Given the paucity of empirical evidence on the issue, the evidence on savings responses in general, and the theory outlined above, it appears difficult to argue for repeal of the estate tax to increase private saving. Even if the responsiveness to the estate and gift tax is as large as the largest empirical estimates of interest elasticities, the effect on savings and output would be negligible and more than offset by public dissaving.[14] Indeed, if the only objective were increased savings, it would probably be more effective to simply keep the estate and gift tax and use the proceeds to reduce the national debt.

Effect on Farms and Closely Held Businesses

Much attention been focused on the effect of the estate and gift tax on family farms and businesses and there is a perception that the estate tax is a significant burden on these businesses. Typically, family farm and business owners hold significant wealth in business and farm assets as well as other assets such as stocks, bonds and cash. Because many business owners are relatively well off and the estate and gift tax is a progressive tax, the probability of a farm or small business owner encountering tax liability is greater than for other decedents.[15]

Opponents of the estate and gift tax suggest that a family business or farm may in fact have to sell assets, often at a discounted price, to pay the tax. In his 1997 testimony, Bruce Bartlett from the National Center for Policy Analysis, stated that:

> according to a survey, 51% of businesses would have difficulty surviving in the event of principal owner's death and 14% said it would be impossible for them to survive. Only 10% said the estate tax would have no effect; 30% said they would have to sell the family business, and 41% would have to borrow against equity.[16]

Are the data from this survey representative of the country as a whole? And, what are the policy issues associated with this effect? In response to the above testimony, there are two questions to explore. One, is repeal of the estate and gift tax efficiently targeted to relieve farms and small businesses?

And two, of the farmer and small business decedents, how many actually encounter estate tax liability?

Target Efficiency

Congress has incorporated into tax law provisions, outlined earlier, that address and reduce the negative consequences of the estate tax on farms and small businesses. These laws are targeted to benefit only farm and small business heirs. In contrast, proposals to repeal the estate and gift tax entirely are poorly targeted to farms and small businesses.

Of the 17,416 taxable returns filed in 2007, 1,137 (6.5%) included farm assets. Additionally, no more than 8,291 (47.6%) returns included "business assets" in the estate.[17] (Note that some returns are double counted.) Together, farm and business owners, by our definition, represent approximately 54.1% of all taxable estate tax returns.[18]

However, this estimate is dramatically overstated, even aside from the likelihood of double counting. The estimate for farms assumes any estate with a farm asset is a farm return thus including part-time farmers or those who may own farm land not directly farmed. The estimate for business assets may include many returns that include small interests (particularly for corporate stock and partnerships). Treasury data for 1998 indicated that farm estates where farm assets accounted for at least half of the gross estate accounted for 1.4% of taxable estates, while returns with closely held stock, non-corporate business or partnership assets equal to half of the gross estate accounted for 1.6%. The same data indicated that farm real estate and other farm assets in these returns accounted for 0.6% of the gross value of estates. Similarly estates with half of the assets representing business assets accounted for 4.1% of estates' gross values. Thus, it is clear that if the main motive for repealing the estate tax or reducing rates across-the-board were to assist farms and small businesses, most of the revenue loss would accrue to those outside the target group.

How Many Farm and Small Business Decedents Pay the Tax?

The more difficult question to answer is how many decedent farmers and small family business owners pay the tax. The first step in answering this question is to estimate the number of farmers and business owners (or those with farm and business assets) who die in any given year. We chose 2005 as our base year.

About 2.4 million people 25 and over died in the United States in 2005.[19] Some portion were farm and business owners. To estimate the number of those who died that were farm or business owners, we assume that the distribution of income tax filers roughly approximates the distribution of deaths in any given year. Or, the portion of farm individual income tax returns to total income tax returns in 2004 approximates the number farm deaths to total deaths. The same logic is used to approximate the number of business owner deaths. (Note that farmers tend to be older than other occupational groups and have somewhat higher death rates, which may slightly overstate our estimates of the share of farmer estates with tax.)

In 2005, there were 134.4 million individual income tax returns filed; about 2 million were classified as farm returns and about 21 million included business income or loss. These returns represent 1.5% and 15.7% of all returns respectively. If the profile of individual income tax return filers is similar to the profile of decedents, this implies approximately 36,720 farmers and 384,339 business owners died in 2005.[20]

Recall that the estate tax return data include 1,137 taxable returns with farm assets and 8,291 taxable returns we classify as business returns. Dividing these two numbers by the estimated number of deaths for each vocation yields an taxable estate tax return rate of 2.1% for farm owner decedents and 2.4% for business owner decedents. Thus, one can conclude that most farmers and business owners are unlikely to encounter estate tax liability.

Other Issues

Liquidity constraints or the inability of farms and small business to meet their tax liability with cash, may not be widespread. A CBO analysis of 1999 and 2000 estate tax data indicated that between 8% and 12% of estates with farm assets owed estate taxes greater than their liquid assets, compared to 5% for all estates that owed estate taxes. Similarly, CBO found that nearly one-third of small businesses that claim the qualified family-owned business-interest deduction owe estate taxes greater than their liquid assets.[21]

Further, estimates using 1992 data suggest that 41% of business owners could pay estate and gift taxes solely out of narrowly defined liquid assets (insurance proceeds, cash and bank accounts); if stocks (equities) were included in a business's liquid assets, an estimated 54% could cover their estate and gift tax liability; if bonds are included an estimated 58% could cover their tax.[22]

These estimates suggest that only 3% to 4% of family farms and businesses would potentially be at risk even without accounting for the special exemptions; the special exemption suggests a much smaller number would be at risk.[23] If one included other non-business assets that are either not included in these estimates through lack of data (such as pensions) or nonfinancial assets (such as real estate) the estimate would be even higher. For many businesses a partial sale of assets (e.g., a portion of farm land) might be made or business assets could be used as security for loans to pay the tax. Finally, some estates may wish to liquidate the business because no heir wishes to continue it. Given these studies and analysis, it appears that only a tiny fraction, almost certainly no more than a percent or so, of heirs of business owners and farmers would be at risk of being forced to liquidate the family business to pay estate and gift taxes.

Effects of the Marital Deduction

One of the most important deductions from the estate tax is the unlimited marital deduction, which accounted for 30.6% of the gross value of all estates, and over 37% for larger estates (see Table 3; larger estates may be more likely to reflect the death of the first spouse). An individual can leave his or her entire estate to a surviving spouse without paying any tax and getting step-up in basis (which permits no tax on accrued gains). The arguments for an unlimited marital deduction are obvious: since spouses tend to be relatively close in age, taxing wealth transferred between spouses amounts to a "double tax" in a generation and also discourages the adequate provision for the surviving spouse (although this latter objective could be met with a large, but not necessarily unlimited, marital deduction). (There is, however, a partial credit for prior transfers within a decade which could mitigate this double taxation within a generation.) Moreover, without an exclusion for assets transferred to the spouse, a substantial amount of planning early in the married couple's life (e.g., allowing for joint ownership of assets) could make a substantial difference in the estate tax liability.

Nevertheless, the unlimited marital deduction causes a certain amount of distortion. If a spouse leaves all assets to the surviving spouse, he or she forgoes the unified credit, equivalent to an exclusion that is currently $3.5 million in 2009. In addition, because the estate tax is graduated, leaving all assets to a spouse can cause the couple to lose the advantage of going through the lower rate brackets twice. A very wealthy donor would leave enough to children (or to the ultimate beneficiary after the second spouse's death) to cover the exemption and to go through all of the rate brackets; then when the second spouse dies, another exemption and another "walk through the rate brackets" will be available. Donors can try to avoid the loss of these benefits and still provide for the surviving spouse by setting up trusts to allow lifetime income to the spouse and perhaps provide for invasion of the corpus for emergencies. These methods, of course, require pre-planning and may not be perfect substitutes for simply leaving assets to the surviving spouse, who would not have complete control.

Under other circumstances, the unlimited marital deduction can cause a decedent to leave more wealth to his or her spouse than would otherwise be preferable. For example, a decedent with children from a previous marriage might like to leave more assets to the children but the unlimited marital deduction may make it more attractive to leave assets to a spouse. One way of dealing with this problem is to leave a lifetime interest to the spouse and direct the disposal of the corpus of the trust to children. Indeed, the tax law facilitates this approach by allowing a trust called a Qualified Terminable Interest Property (QTIP) trust. Nevertheless, this approach also requires planning and is not a perfect substitute for directly leaving assets to children (particularly if the spouse has a long prospective life).

The point is that these provisions, whether deemed desirable or undesirable, distort the choices of a decedent and cause more resources to be devoted to estate planning than would otherwise be the case.

A Backstop for the Income Tax

Capital Gains

One reason frequently cited by tax analysts for retaining an estate tax is that the tax acts as a back-up for a source of leakage in the individual income tax—the failure to tax capital gains passed on at death. Normally, a capital gains tax applies on the difference between the sales price of an asset and the cost of acquiring it (this cost is referred to as the basis). Under current law, accumulated capital gains on an asset held until death will never be subject to the capital gains tax because the heirs will treat the market value at time of death (rather than original cost) as their basis. Assuming market values are estimated correctly, if heirs immediately sold these assets, no tax would be due. This treatment is referred to as "step-up in basis." It is estimated that 36% or more of gains escape taxes through step-up.[24]

The estate and gift tax is not a carefully designed back-up for the capital gains tax. It allows no deduction for original cost basis, it has large exemptions which may exclude much of capital gains from the tax in any case (including the unlimited marital deduction), and the tax rates vary from those that would be imposed on capital gains if realized. In particular, estate tax rates can be much larger than those imposed on capital gains (the current capital gains tax is capped at 20%, while the maximum marginal estate tax rate is 45%).

If the capital gains tax were the primary reason for retaining an estate and gift tax, then the tax could be restructured to impose capital gains taxes on a constructive realization basis. Alternatively, one could adopt a carry-over of basis, so that the basis remained the original cost, although this proposal could still allow an indefinite deferral of gain.

Owner-Occupied Housing, Life Insurance, and Other Assets

Owner occupied housing and life insurance also escape income taxes on capital gains accrued through inside build-up (for the most part). Owner-occupied housing also escapes income tax on implicit rental income. There are practical economic and administrative reasons for some of these tax rules. It is administratively difficult to tax implicit rental income and taxing capital gains could potentially impede labor mobility. There are other assets as well that escape the income tax (such as tax exempt bonds). The estate and gift tax could also be seen as a backstop for these lapses in the individual income tax.

Effects of the Charitable Deduction

One group that benefits from the presence of an estate and gift tax is the non-profit sector, since charitable contributions can be given or bequeathed without paying tax. As shown in Table 3, estates that filed returns in 2007 donated 9.7% of total assets to charities; estates that occupy the highest wealth class ($20 million or greater) donated 21.2% of total assets to charity. Although one recent study found that charitable bequests are very responsive to the estate tax, and indeed that the charitable deduction is "target efficient" in the sense that it induces more charitable contributions than it loses in revenue, other studies have found a variety of responses, both small and large.[25] One problem with these types of studies is the difficulty in separating wealth and price effects.

An individual would have even greater tax benefits if charitable contributions were made during the lifetime, since they are deductible for purposes of the income tax, thereby reducing not only income tax but also, because the eventual estate is reduced, the estate tax as well. On the other hand, under the income tax charitable gifts are limited to 50% of income (30% for private foundations) and there are also restrictions on the ability to deduct appreciated property at full value. Despite this effect, a significant amount of charitable giving occurs through bequests and one study estimated that total charitable giving through bequests would fall by 12% if the estate tax were eliminated.[26] This reduction is, however, less than 1% of total charitable contributions.[27]

Charitable deductions play a role in some estate planning techniques described in the next section. In addition, some charitable deductions allow considerable retention of control by the heirs, as in the case of private foundations. Unlike the case of the income tax, there are no special restrictions on bequests to private foundations. (Under the income tax system, deductibility as a percent of income is more limited for gifts to foundations; there are also more limitations on gifts of appreciated property to foundations.)[28]

Efficiency Effects, Distortions, and Administrative Costs

A number of tax planning and tax avoidance techniques take advantage of the annual gift exclusion, the charitable deduction, the unlimited marital deduction, and issues of valuation. Because choices made with respect to these techniques can affect total tax liability, these planning techniques complicate compliance on the part of the taxpayer and administration on the part of the IRS. They may also induce individuals to arrange their affairs in ways that would not otherwise be desirable, resulting in distortions of economic behavior.

The most straightforward method of reducing estate and gift taxes is to transfer assets as gifts during the lifetime (inter-vivos transfers) rather than bequests. Gifts are generally subject to lower taxes for two reasons. First, assets can be transferred without affecting the unified credit because of the $12,000 annual exclusion. The exclusion was designed to permit gifts (such as wedding and Christmas presents) without involving the complication of the gift tax. This annual exclusion can, however, allow very large lifetime gifts. For example, a couple with two children, who are both married, could make $96,000 of tax-free gifts per year (each spouse could give $12,000 to each child and the child's spouse). Over 10 years, $960,000 could be transferred tax free (and without reducing the lifetime credit). Moreover, the estate is further reduced by the appreciation on these assets.

The effective gift tax is also lower than the estate tax because it is imposed on a tax-exclusive basis rather than a tax-inclusive basis. For example, if the tax rate is 45%, a taxable gift (beyond the $12,000 limit) of $100,000 can be given with a $45,000 gift tax, for an out-of-pocket total cost to the decedent of $145,000. However, if the transfer were made at death, the estate tax on the total outlay of $145,000 would be 45% of the total, or $65,250. Despite these significant advantages, especially from the annual exclusion, relatively little inter-vivos giving occurs.[29] There are a number of possible reasons for this failure to take advantage of the gift exclusion, and one is that the donee does not wish to relinquish economic control or perhaps provide assets to children before they are deemed to have sufficient maturity to handle them. There are certain trust and other devices that have been developed to allow some control to be maintained while utilizing the annual gift tax exclusion.[30] The annual gift exclusion can also be used to shift the ownership of insurance policies away from the person whose life is insured and out of the gross estate.

One particular method that allows a potentially large amount of estate tax avoidance is a Crummey trust. Normally, gifts placed in a trust are not eligible for the $12,000 exclusion, unless the trust allows a present interest by the beneficiary. The courts have held that contributions to a trust that allows the beneficiary withdrawal rights, even if the individual is a minor, and even if withdrawal rights are available for only a brief period (e.g.,15 or 30 days), can be treated as gifts eligible for the annual exclusion. This rule has been used to remove insurance assets from an estate (by placing them in a trust and using the annual $12,000 gift exclusion to pay the premiums without incurring tax). Under the Crummey trust, a large number of individuals (who may be children or other relatives of the primary beneficiaries) can be given the right (a right not usually exercised) to withdraw up to $12,000 over the limited time period. (Under lapse of power rules, however, this amount is sometimes limited to $6,000.) All of these individuals are not necessarily primary beneficiaries of the trust but they expand the gift exclusion aggregate. In one case, a Crummey trust with 35 donees was reported.[31]

There is, however, one disadvantage of inter vivos gifts: these gifts do not benefit from the step-up in basis at death that allows capital gains to go unrecognized, so that very wealthy families with assets with large unrealized gains might prefer bequests (at least after the annual exclusion is used up).[32]

Individuals can also avoid taxes by skipping generations; although there is a generation skipping tax, there are large exemptions from the tax ($3.5 million per decedent in 2009, the same as the general estate tax exemption amount). Generation skipping may be accomplished through a direct skip (a decedent leaves assets to grandchildren rather than children) or an indirect skip (assets are left in a trust with income rights to children, and the corpus passing to the grandchildren on the children's death). The generation skipping tax rate is 45%. Relatively little revenue has been collected from the generation skipping tax because the tax has been successful in eliminating generation skipping transfers that are above the limit.[33]

Charitable deductions can also be used to avoid estate and gift taxes (and income taxes as well). For example, if a charity can be given rights to an asset during a fixed period (through a fixed annuity, or a fixed percentage of the asset's value), with the remainder going to the donor's children or other heirs, estate taxes can be avoided if the period of the trust is overstated (by being based on a particular individual life that is likely to be shorter than the actuarial life). Although restrictions have now been applied to limit reference persons to related parties, in the past so-called "vulture trusts" that recruited a completely unrelated person with a diminished life expectancy were used to avoid tax.[34]

Assets can also be transferred to charity while maintaining control through private foundations. Private foundations allow an individual or his or her heirs to direct the disposition of funds in the foundations for charitable purposes and continue to exercise power and control over the assets.

As noted earlier, some estate planning techniques are used to provide maximum benefits of the marital deduction plus the exclusion and lower rates; these approaches can also involve the use of trusts, such as the Qualified Terminable Interest Property (QTIP). These plans may permit the invasion of the corpus for emergency reasons.

Finally, a significant way of reducing estate taxes is to reduce the valuation of assets. A lower valuation can be achieved by transferring assets into a family partnership with many interests so that one party is not technically able to sell at a "market price" without agreement from the other owners to sell, a circumstance that the courts have seen as lowering the value of even obviously marketable assets, such as publicly traded stocks (the minority interest discount). Undervaluation can also be argued through the claim that a sale of a large block of stock (a "fire sale") would reduce asset value or, with a family-owned business, that the death of the owner (or a "key man") lowers the value substantially. A fractional interest in a property (such as real estate) may also qualify for a discount. Discounts may also be allowed for special use property whose market value may be higher than the value of the property in its current use.

Estate planning techniques complicate the tax law, increase the resources in the economy devoted to planning and also increase the administrative burden on the IRS especially when such cases go to court. Some claims have been made that the administrative costs and costs to taxpayers comprise a large part of the revenues. However, a recent study set the costs of complying with the estate tax at 6 to 9% of revenues. Moreover, an interesting argument was also made in that study that the inducement to settle affairs provided by the existence of an estate tax may be beneficial as it encourages individuals to get their affairs in order and avoid costly and difficult disputes among heirs.[35]

Of course, the administrative and compliance costs are, themselves, in part a consequence of the design of the tax. If the estate tax were revised to mitigate some of the need for tax planning, the administrative and compliance costs might be lower.

The high tax rates for some estates and the lack of third-party reporting mechanisms suggest that compliance may be a problem, although a large fraction of returns with large estates are audited. Estimates of the estate "tax gap," or the fraction of revenues that are not collected, have varied considerably; a recent estimate suggests about 31% of estates and gift taxes are not collected, although the authors of previous estimates suggest that this measure is very difficult to estimate.[36]

Repeal of Federal Credit for State Estate and Inheritance Taxes

In theory, the federal credit for state death taxes eliminated the incentive for states to "race to the bottom" of state estate tax rates and burden. Lower state liability simply increased federal liability by an equal amount. In short, the state credit was simply a federal transfer to states contingent upon the state's maintenance of an estate tax. The credit also reduced the federal tax burden of the estate and gift tax. The highest effective credit rate was of 16% of the gross estate value which reduced the highest federal rate of 55% to 39% (before EGTRRA).

In 2005, the "credit for state death taxes" was eliminated and replaced with a deduction for those taxes. Many states have relied on the federal credit for their estate tax and will need to modify their tax laws to continue collecting their estate and inheritance taxes. Under current state laws, "... there will be 29 states that have no state death tax in 2005."[37]

POLICY OPTIONS

Repealing the Estate and Gift Tax

One option is to eliminate the estate tax. This approach has been taken in the 2001 tax cut bill, the Economic Growth and Tax Relief Reconciliation Act of 2001 (EGTRRA, P.L. 107-16). However, the legislation sunsets after 2010, reverting to what the law would have been in 2011 if not for EGTRRA. During the phase-out period, the estate tax will still generate revenue, thus understating the full fiscal impact (revenue loss) of complete repeal. Immediate repeal of the estate and gift tax would cost up to $662 billion, whereas the estimated 10-year revenue cost of the temporary repeal of the estate tax under EGTRRA was $138 billion.

The Bush Administration's FY2009 budget proposal contained a proposal to permanently repeal the estate and gift tax beginning in 2010 by repealing the EGTRRA sunset. The revenue loss from that proposal would have been $522 billion over the 2009-2018 budget window. Most of the revenue loss would have accrued in the out years of the proposal; from 2014 to 2018, the proposal would cost $372.3 billion in lost federal revenue.

Increasing the Credit, Converting to an Exemption, and/or Changing Rates

Several of the compromise proposals mentioned earlier in this report would both increase the exemption (eliminating the credit structure) amount and lower the rate. For example in the 110th Congress, H.R. 3170 would have set the exemption at $5 million for each spouse ($10 million per couple) and lowered the tax rate to 35%, while H.R. 4235 would have set the exemption at $3 million per decedent and reduced marginal estate tax rates by 20%. No potential revenue loss estimates were available for either proposal.

Taxing the Capital Gains of Heirs vs. the Estate Tax

In 2010, the estate tax will be replaced by a tax on the capital gains of heirs when an inherited asset is sold. The new law will include an exemption from carryover basis for capital gains of $1.3 million (and an additional $3 million for a surviving spouse). There are efficiency losses to taxing capital gains of heirs on inherited assets because such taxation would increase the lock-in effect. The lock-in effect occurs when potential taxpayers hold onto their assets because of the anticipated tax on the gain. If the asset value grows from generation to generation, the lock-in effect becomes stronger and stronger. Some analysts have suggested that the result of the lock-in effect will be familial asset hoarding. Legislation that repeals the EGTRRA sunset would retain this treatment of capital gains.

Both taxation of gains at death and carry-over basis may be complicated by lack of information by the executor on the basis of assets (some of which may have been originally inherited by the decedent). Indeed, a proposal in the 1970s to provide carry-over basis was never put into place because of protests, some associated with the problem of determining the basis. This problem may be less serious for EGTRRA because of the carry-over of basis exemption.

Allowing constructive realization or carryover basis may further complicate estate planning if an exemption were allowed, because it would be advantageous to pick those assets with the largest amounts of appreciation for the exclusion or carryover basis. In addition, since the tax arising from carryover basis would depend on the heir's income tax rates, revenues could be saved by allocating appreciated assets to heirs with the lowest expected tax rates.

Changing from the current step-up basis for inherited assets to a carryover basis, as enacted by EGTRRA, will also affect the life insurance choices of taxpayers. Generally, EGTRRA will likely encourage taxpayers to invest more in life insurance than other investments. Under current tax law, the appreciation of assets held in life insurance policies is not subject to capital gains taxes. Also, the payout from these policies, usually in cash to heirs, is not subject to income taxes and effectively receives a stepped up basis. The switch to carryover basis at death would then favor life insurance policies over other assets that are subject to capital gains taxes at death (assuming the heir liquidates the assets). The anticipated change to more assets held in life insurance policies will likely reduce the revenue generated by capital gains taxes.

Concerns of Farms and Family Businesses

If the estate tax is not repealed, farms and family businesses may be targeted for further relief by increases in the special exemptions for farm and business assets.[38] Because of the asset distribution of estates, almost all decedents with significant farm or business assets would likely not pay an estate tax. While this approach would be effective at targeting family farms and businesses for relief, it would exacerbate a general concern with the estate and gift tax—the unfairness of a differential treatment of owners of these business and farm assets compared to those with other forms of assets. Why should a wealthy individual whose assets are in a closely held corporation escape estate and gift tax on his or her assets, while an individual who holds shares in a publicly traded corporation pay a tax?

Larger exemptions also encourage wealthy decedents to convert other property into business or farm property to take advantage of the special exemptions. An incentive already exists to shift property into this exempt form and it would have been exacerbated by an expansion of the exemption.

Reform Proposals and Other Structural Changes

Many pre-EGTRRA proposals were intended to modify rather than completely repeal the estate tax. Some of these proposals may be revisited as the sunset provision in EGTRRA nears. The proposed revisions would have focused on eliminating estate tax avoidance schemes or at fixing current inconsistencies in the estate tax law. The issues presented here are still relevant for both because the gift tax is retained even after eventual repeal of the estate tax and because the estate tax may be retained under legislative proposals.

Phase out of Unified Credit for Largest Estates

This provision would allow for a phase out of the unified credit as well as the lower rates, by extending the bubble. This provision would cause all assets in large estates to be taxed at the top rate of 45%.

Impose Consistent Valuation Rules

Analysts have proposed that valuation of assets be the same for income tax purposes as for estate tax purposes. Basically, it is advantageous to *overvalue* assets for purposes of the income tax, so as to minimize any future capital gains tax liability. Conversely, its advantageous to *undervalue* assets to minimize estate tax liability. In addition to requiring consistency in valuation, some have proposed that donors report the basis of assets given as gifts. Currently, assets transferred by gift and then sold do not benefit from step-up in basis even though the donor is not required to report the basis to the donee. A requirement for consistent valuation rules was included in President Obama's budget proposals.[39]

Modify the Rules for the Allocation of Basis

Under current law, a transaction that is part gift and part sale assigns a basis to the asset for the donee that is the larger of the fair market value or the amount actually paid. The donor pays a tax on the difference between amount paid and his basis and may frequently recognize no gain. This proposal would allocate basis proportionally to the gift and sale portions.[40]

Eliminate Stepped up Basis on Survivor's Share of Community Property

Under present law, in common law states, half of property held jointly by a married couple is included in the first decedent's gross estate and that half is thus eligible for step-up in basis for purposes of future capital gains. In community property states, however, where all properties acquired during marriage are deemed community property, a step up in basis is available for all community property, not just the half that is allocated to the decedent spouse. The reason for this rule, which is quite old, was the presumption in the past that property in a common law state would have been held by the husband (who would have acquired it) and thus would all have been eligible for step-up, while only one half of property in community property states would have been deemed to be held by the husband and be eligible for step up. This older treatment, it is argued, was made obsolete by changes in 1981 that determined that only half of any jointly held property would be included in the estate regardless of how the property was acquired, and thus made the step up apply to only one half of this type of property. Thus, currently couples in community property states are being treated more favorably than those in common law states.

A reservation with this treatment is that property that could be allocated to one spouse in a common law state may not be able to escape the community property treatment in a community property states, and common law states may now be favored if these assets in common law states tend to be held by the first decedent. However, couples in community property states may be able to convert to separate property by agreement, and thereby take advantage of the same planning opportunities as those in common law states.

Modify QTIP Rules

Under present law, an individual may obtain a marital deduction for amounts left in trust to a spouse under a Qualified Terminable Interest Property (QTIP) trust, with one requirement being that the second spouse must then include the trust amounts in their own estate. In some cases the second estate has argued that there is a defect in the trust arrangement so that the trust amount is not included in the second spouse's estate (even though a deduction was allowed for it in the first spouse's estate). This provision would require inclusion in the second spouse's estate for any amount excluded in the first spouse's estate.

Eliminate Non-Business Valuation Discount

This provision would require that marketable assets be valued at the fair market value (i.e., there would be no valuation discounts for holding assets in a family partnership or for "fire-sale" dispositions). A revision of this type was included in President Obama's budget proposals.[41]

Eliminate the Exception for a Retained Interest in Personal Residences from Gift Tax Rules

Under current law, when a gift is made but the grantor retains an interest, that retained interest is valued at zero (making the size of the gift and the gift tax larger). In the case of a personal residence, however, the retained interest is valued based on actuarial tables. In general, retained interests are only allowed to be deducted from the fair market of the gift (reducing gift taxes) if they can be objectively valued (and hence are allowed for certain types of trusts, such as those that pay an annuity).

Disallow Annual Gift Taxes in a Crummey Trust

As noted earlier, the annual gift exclusion is not available for gifts placed in trust unless certain rules are met, but a Crummey trust, which allows some right of withdrawal, is eligible. This revision would allow gifts in trust to be deductible only if the only beneficiary is the individual, and if the trust does not terminate before the individual dies, the assets will be in the beneficiary's estate. These rules are similar to generation skipping taxes.

Reduce the Annual Gift Tax Exclusion

The annual gift tax exclusion allows significant amounts to be transferred free of tax and also plays a role in transferring insurance out of the estate (by using the annual gift tax exclusion to pay the premium). While some gift tax exclusion is probably desirable for simplification purposes, the $12,000 exclusion's role in estate tax avoidance could be reduced by reducing its size. An alternative change that would limit the use of the annual exclusion in tax avoidance approaches would be a single exclusion per donor (or some aggregate limit per donor), to prevent the multiplication of the excluded amount by gifts to several children and those children's spouses and the use of techniques such as the Crummey trust.

Allow Inheritance of Marital Deductions or Lower Rates

One of the complications of estate planning is maximizing the use of the exemption and lower rate brackets by a married couple. In this case, while it may be economically and personally desirable to pass the entire estate (or most of the estate) to the surviving spouse, minimizing taxes would require passing to others at least the exemption amount and perhaps more to take some advantage as well of the lower rate brackets. Such complex situations could be avoided by allowing the surviving spouse to inherit any unused deduction and lower rate brackets so that the couple's full deductions and lower rates could be utilized regardless of how much was left to the surviving spouse.

Allow Gift Tax Treatment Only on Final and Actual Transfer

Many of the tax avoidance techniques with charitable gifts involve over-valuation of a deductible interest. For example, a gift may be made of the remainder interest after an annuity has been provided to a charitable organization . The larger the value of the charitable annuity, the smaller the value of the gift (and the gift tax). One way to over-value an annuity is to allow the annuity to extend to a particular individual's lifetime, when that individual has a shorter life than the actuarial tables indicate. Similarly, a way to transfer income via the gift tax exclusion without the recipient having control over it is to place it in a Crummey trust. Even if the individual is able to exercise withdrawal rights, the expectation of not receiving future gifts if the assets are withdrawn in violation of the donor's wishes may mean that such rights will never be exercised. A rule that excludes all assets placed in trusts from consideration for the gift tax would eliminate this mechanism.

These types of valuation techniques could be addressed by only allowing the gift tax to be imposed at the time of the actual final transfer. In such a case, no actuarial valuation would be necessary and no trust mechanisms would be available.

Valuation of Assets

One option is to disallow discounts for property that has a market value (such as bonds and publicly traded stock) regardless of the form the asset is held in, as suggested by the administration tax proposals. Such a change would prevent the avoidance technique of placing assets into a family partnership or similar arrangement and then arguing that the property has lost market value because it would require agreement of the heirs to sell it. In addition, other limits on valuation discounts could be imposed. For example, blockage discounts based on "fire sale" arguments could be disallowed. Such a provision might allow for an adjustment if the property is immediately sold at such a lower price.

Include Life Insurance Proceeds in the Base

Some tax avoidance techniques are associated with shifting life insurance proceeds out of the estate by shifting to another owner.

Switch to an Inheritance Tax

Some authors have suggested that an inheritance tax should be substituted for the estate tax. Some states have inheritance taxes. An estate tax applies to the total assets left by the decedent. An inheritance tax would be applied separately to assets received by each of the heirs. If tax rates are progressive, smaller taxes would be applied the greater the number of beneficiaries of the assets. One reason for such a change would, therefore, be to encourage more dispersion of wealth among heirs, since taxes would be lower (assuming exemptions and graduated rates) if split among more recipients. In addition, under an inheritance tax the tax rate can be varied according to the status of the heir (son vs. cousin, for example). At the same time, one can see more avoidance complications arising from an inheritance tax.

CONCLUSION

The analysis in this report has suggested that some of the arguments used for and against maintaining the estate tax may be questioned or of lesser import than is popularly assumed. For example, there is little evidence that the estate tax has much effect on savings (and therefore on output); indeed, estate taxes could easily increase rather than reduce savings. Similarly, only a tiny fraction of farms and small businesses face the estate and gift tax and it has been estimated that the majority of those who do have sufficient non-business assets to pay the tax. Moreover, only a small potion of the estate tax is collected from these family owned farms and small businesses, so that dramatically reducing estate tax rates or eliminating the tax for the purpose of helping these family businesses is not very target efficient.

Although the estate tax does contribute to the progressivity of the tax system, this progressivity is undermined, to an undetermined degree, by certain estate tax avoidance techniques. Of course, one alternative is to broaden the estate tax base by restricting some of these estate planning techniques. At the same time progressivity could be achieved by other methods.

On the other hand, arguments that the estate tax is a back-up for the income escaping the capital gains tax, would not support the current high rates of the estate tax, which should be lowered to 20% or less to serve this purpose.

More intangible arguments, such as the argument that inheritances are windfalls that should be taxed at higher rates on the one hand, or that death is an undesirable time to levy a tax and that transferred assets have already been subject to taxes, are more difficult to assess but remain important issues in the determination of the desirability of estate and gift taxes.

Appendix. Estate and Gift Tax Data

Table A-1. The Filing Requirement and Unified Credit

Year of Death	Filing Requirement or Equivalent Exemption	Unified Credit
2004 and 2005	$1,500,000	$555,800
2006 through 2008	$2,000,000	$780,800
2009	$3,500,000	$1,525,800
2010	estate tax repealed	estate tax repealed
2011 and after	$1,000,000	$345,800

Table A-2. Gross Estate Value for Returns Filed in 2007

All Returns	Taxable Returns	Gross Estate Value All Returns (in $ 000s)	Gross Estate Value Taxable Returns (in $ 000s)	Percent Taxable Estate Tax Returns
38,031	17,416	203,095,593	112,164,528	45.8%
19,806	8,483	51,481,033	22,582,887	42.8%
5,943	2,860	24,484,232	11,766,752	48.1%
5,429	2,906	36,774,179	19,797,158	53.5%
1,892	1,104	25,673,363	15,075,868	58.4%
1,017	654	58,374,979	40,605,379	64.3%

Source: Internal Revenue Service, Statistics of Income, *Estate Tax Returns Filed in 2007*, IRS, SOI unpublished data, October 2008.

Table A-3. Allowable Deductions on 2007 Returns (Sorted by Total Value)

Deduction	Returns with Deduction		Value of Deductions (in $ 000s)	
	Total	Taxable	Total	Taxable
Total deductions	37,997	17,406	93,245,904	30,272,872
Bequests to surviving spouse	17,422	1,585	62,056,974	11,175,806
Charitable deductions	7,672	4,254	19,701,929	12,229,881
Debts and mortgages	27,874	15,352	7,624,009	3,757,752
Executor's commissions	13,042	10,388	1,273,483	1,100,072
Other expenses and losses	23,336	14,894	1,140,019	976,226
Attorney's fees	23,175	14,880	915,224	703,937
Funeral expenses	32,960	16,618	340,616	167,972
State death taxes paid	11,608	7,841	3,394,074	3,095,495

Source: Internal Revenue Service, Statistics of Income, Estate Tax Returns Filed in *2007*, IRS, SOI unpublished data, October 2008.

Table A-4. 2009 Estate Tax Rate Schedule

Taxable Estate Value From	to	Current Statutory Rate (in Percent)
$0	$10,000	18
$10,001	$20,000	20
$20,001	$40,000	22
$40,001	$60,000	24
$60,001	$80,000	26
$80,001	$100,000	28
$100,001	$150,000	30
$150,001	$250,000	32
$250,001	$500,000	34
$500,001	$750,000	37
$750,001	$1,000,000	39
$1,000,001	$1,250,000	41
$1,250,001	$1,500,000	43
$1,500,001	and over	45

Table A-5. Repealed Credit for State Death Taxes

Taxable Estate Value (less the $60,000 exemption)	to	Current Statutory Credit Rate (in Percent)
$0	$40,000	0
$40,001	$90,000	.8
$90,001	$140,000	1.6
$140,001	$240,000	2.4
$240,001	$440,000	3.2
$440,001	$640,000	4.0
$640,001	$840,000	4.8
$840,001	$1,040,000	5.6
$1,040,001	$1,540,000	6.4
$1,540,001	$2,040,000	7.2
$2,040,001	$2,540,000	8.0

Table A-5. (Continued).

Taxable Estate Value (less the $60,000 exemption)	to	Current Statutory Credit Rate (in Percent)
$2,540,001	$3,040,000	8.8
$3,040,001	$3,540,000	9.6
$3,540,001	$4,040,000	10.4
$4,040,001	$5,040,000	11.2
$5,040,001	$6,040,000	12.0
$6,040,001	$7,040,000	12.8
$7,040,001	$8,040,000	13.6
$8,040,001	$9,040,000	14.4
$9,040,001	$10,040,000	15.2

Note: In 2005, the credit was repealed and replaced with a deduction.

Table A-6. Wealth Distribution of Taxable Returns Filed in 2007

Size of Gross Estate	Taxable Returns	Gross Taxable Estate Value (in $ 000s)	Net Estate Tax (in $ 000s)	Percent of Taxable Estate Returns	Percent Gross Taxable Estate Tax Value
All Returns	17,416	112,164,528	22,508,292	100.00%	100.00%
2.0 to 3.5 million	8,483	22,582,887	2,352,847	48.71%	20.13%
3.5 to 5.0 million	2,860	11,766,752	2,371,313	16.42%	10.49%
5.0 to 10.0 million	2,906	19,797,158	5,173,865	16.69%	17.65%
10.0 to 20 million	1,104	15,075,868	4,445,947	6.34%	13.44%
over 20.0 million	654	40,605,379	8,027,849	3.76%	36.20%

Source: Internal Revenue Service, Statistics of Income, *Estate Tax Returns Filed in 2007*, IRS, SOI unpublished data, October 2008.

End Notes

[1] U.S. Department of the Treasury, General Explanations of the Administration's Fiscal Year 2009 Revenue Proposals, Washington, Feb. 2008, p. 129.

[2] See CRS Report R40615, Estate and Gift Tax Revenues: Past and Projected in 2009, by Nonna A. Noto, p. 20, for year by year estimates.

[3] Possible consequences that have been discussed include concentrations of political power, inefficient investments by the very wealthy, and disincentives to work by heirs (often referred to as the Carnegie conjecture, reflecting a claim argued by Andrew Carnegie).

[4] For a history of the estate and gift tax as well as a detailed explanation of current law, see the following CRS reports by John R. Luckey: CRS Report 95-416, Federal Estate, Gift, and Generation-Skipping Taxes: A Description of Current Law, and CRS Report 95-444, A History of Federal Estate, Gift, and Generation-Skipping Taxes.

[5] 26 I.R.C. 2001(c).

[6] The federal credit for state death taxes paid was repealed beginning in 2005. See Table A-4 in the Appendix for the old credit for state death taxes paid schedule.

[7] We have dropped the modifier "adjusted" from taxable estate for the benefit of the reader. The taxable estate and the adjusted taxable estate are identical in the absence of taxable gifts.

[8] The data are from those estates that filed in 2006, thus some estates followed the 2004 rules which still included the credit for state death taxes.

[9] This is slightly greater than the tentative estate tax less credits because of rounding.

[10] Mortality data for 2005 is the latest year available.

[11] For more see Douglas Holtz-Eakin, David Joulfaian, and Harvey Rosen, "The Carnegie Conjecture: Some Empirical Evidence," Quarterly Journal of Economics, v. 108, May 1993, pp. 413-435.

[12] William G. Gale and Maria G. Perozek. "Do Estate Taxes Reduce Savings?" April 2000. Presented at a Conference on Estate and Gift Taxes sponsored by the Office of Tax Policy Research, University of Michigan, and the Brookings Institution, May 4-5, 2000.

[13] Wojciech Kopczuk and Joel Slemrod, "The Impact of the Estate Tax on the Wealth Accumulation and Avoidance Behavior of Donors," in William G. Gale, James R. Hines Jr., and Joel B. Slemrod, eds., Rethinking Estate and Gift Taxation, pp. 299-343. Washington, DC: Brookings Institution Press, 2001.

[14] Interest elasticities have been estimated at no higher than 0.4; that is, a one percent increase in the rate of return would increase savings by 0.4%. Ignoring the effect on the deficit or assuming the revenue loss is made up by some other tax or spending program that has no effect on private savings, this amount is about 40% of the revenue cost, so that savings might initially increase by about $12 billion. Output would rise by this increase multiplied by the interest rate, or about $1 billion (or, 1/100 of 1% of output). In the long run, savings would accumulate, and national income might eventually increase by about one tenth of 1%. (This calculation is based on the following: the current revenue cost of $28 billion accounts for about 1.4% of capital income of approximately 25% of Net National Product; at an elasticity of 0.4, a 1.4% increase in income would lead to a 0.56 % increase in the capital stock and multiplying by the capital share of income (0.25) would lead to an approximate 0.14 increase in the capital stock.)

[15] See CRS Report RL33070, Estate Taxes and Family Businesses: Economic Issues, by Jane G. Gravelle and Steven Maguire.

[16] Statement before the Subcommittee on Tax, Finance, and Exports, Committee on Small Business, June 12, 1997.

[17] A return is classified as a business return if at least one of the following assets is in the estate: closely held stock, limited partnerships, real estate partnership, other non-corporate business assets. Counting the same estate more than once is likely which significantly overstates the number of business estate tax returns.

[18] See CRS Report RS20593, Asset Distribution of Taxable Estates: An Analysis, by Steven Maguire.

[19] Mortality data for 2005 is the latest year available.

[20] The percentages are multiplied by the 2,448,017 deaths of those 25 years old and over. If the age were higher then the pool of decedents would be smaller and the percentage that paid estate taxes incrementally higher.

[21] U.S. Congressional Budget Office. Effects of the Federal Estate Tax on Farms and Small Businesses. July 2005.

[22] Holtz-Eakin, Douglas, John W. Philips, and Harvey S. Rosen, "Estate Taxes, Life Insurance, and Small Business," Review of Economics and Statistics, v83 n1, 2001.

[23] Of course, if all heirs do not wish to continue ownership in the family business, these liquid assets might need to be used to buy them out; that, however, is a choice made by the heirs and not a forced sale.

[24] See Poterba, James M. and Scott Weisbenner, "The Distributional Burden of Taxing Estates and Unrealized capital Gains at the Time of Death," National Bureau of Economic Research, no. 7811, July 2000, p. 36.

[25] See David Joulfaian, "Estate Taxes and Charitable Bequests by the Wealth," National Tax Journal v53 n3, November 2000. This paper contains a review of the econometric literature on the charitable response. Note that, in general, a tax incentive induces more spending than it loses in revenue when the elasticity (the percentage change in spending divided by the percentage change in taxes) is greater than one.

[26] Ibid.

[27] Bruce Bartlett, Misplaced Fears for Generosity, Washington Times, June 26, 2000, p. A16.

[28] For further discussion and estimates of the effect of estate tax options on charitable giving, see CRS Report R40518, Charitable Contributions: The Itemized Deduction Cap and Other FY2010 Budget Options, by Jane G. Gravelle and Donald J. Marples.

[29] See James Poterba. "Estate and Gift Taxes and Incentives for Inter Vivos Giving in the United States," Journal of Public Economics v79 n1, Jan. 2001. Even at high income levels, Poterba found that only about 45% of households take advantage of lifetime giving. He also found that those with illiquid assets (such as family businesses) and those with large unrealized capital gains are less likely to make inter-vivos gifts.

[30] For a more complete discussion of this and other techniques, see Richard Schmalbeck, "Avoiding Wealth Transfer Taxes," in William G. Gale, James R. Hines Jr., and Joel B. Slemrod, eds., Rethinking Estate and Gift Taxation, pp. 113-163. Washington, DC: Brookings Institution Press, 2001. and Charles Davenport and Jay Soled. Enlivening the Death-Tax Death-Talk. Tax Notes, July 26, 1999, pp. 591-629.

[31] See Davenport and Soled, op cit.

[32] See David Joulfaian, Choosing Between Gifts and Bequests: How Taxes Affect the Timing of Wealth Transfers, National Bureau of Economic Research, Working Paper no. 11025, Jan. 2005.

[33] For a description see CRS Report 95-416, Federal Estate, Gift, and Generation-Skipping Taxes: A Description of Current Law, by John R. Luckey.

[34] See Schmalbeck, op cit. The reference individual cannot be terminal (have a life expectancy of less than a year), however.

[35] See Davenport and Soled, op cit. This study also reviewed a variety of other studies of estate tax compliance costs.

[36] See U.S. Department of The Treasury, Office of Tax Policy, A Comprehensive Strategy for Reducing the Tax Gap, Sept. 26, 2006, p. 6, and Martha Eller, Brian Erard and Chih-Chin Ho, "The Magnitude and Determinants of Federal Estate Tax Noncompliance," in William G. Gale, James R. Hines Jr., and Joel B. Slemrod, eds., Rethinking Estate and Gift Taxation, pp. 375-421. Washington, DC: Brookings Institution Press, 2001.

[37] Harley Duncan, "State Responses to Estate Tax Changes Enacted as Part of the Economic Growth and Tax Relief Reconciliation Act of 2001 (EGTRRA)," State Tax Notes, Dec. 2, 2002, p. 615.

[38] For more on the estate tax and its effect on family businesses, see CRS Report RL33070, Estate Taxes and Family Businesses: Economic Issues, by Jane G. Gravelle and Steven Maguire.

[39] See U.S. Department of Treasury, General Explanation of the Administration's FY2010 Revenue Proposals, May 2009, pp. 119-120, http://www.treas.gov/offices/tax-policy /library/grnbk09.pdf.

[40] For example, suppose an asset with a basis of $50,000 but a market value of $100,000 is sold to the donee for $50,000. The donor would realize no gain and the gift amount would be $50,000, with the donee having a basis of $50,000. Eventually, the gain would be taxed when the donee sold the property, but that tax would be delayed. However, if the asset were divided into a gift of $50,000 with a basis of $25,000 and a sale of $50,000 with a basis of $50,000, the donor would realize a gain of $25,000; the donee would now have a basis of $75,000. Half of the gain would be subject to tax immediately.

[41] See U.S. Department of Treasury, General Explanation of the Administration's FY2010 Revenue Proposals, May 2009, pp. 121-122, http://www.treas.gov/offices/tax-policy/ library/grnbk09.pdf.

In: Estate and Gift Taxes
Editor: Jacob A. Hughes

ISBN: 978-1-62100-516-2

Chapter 2

ESTATE TAX OPTIONS*

Jane G. Gravelle

SUMMARY

The Economic Growth and Tax Relief Reconciliation Act of 2001 (EGTRRA; P.L. 107-16), among other tax cuts, provided for a gradual reduction and elimination of the estate tax. Under EGTRRA, the estate tax exemption rose from $675,000 in 2001 to $3.5 million in 2009, and the rate fell from 55% to 45%. In 2010, the estate tax was eliminated. As with other provisions, however, the estate tax changes were scheduled to sunset in 2011 when the exemption would have become $1 million (as scheduled in pre-EGTRRA law) and the tax rate would return to 55.

There was general agreement that some sort of estate tax would be retained. A proposal to make the 2009 rules ($3.5 million exemption and 45% rate) permanent was included in President Obama's 2010 and 2011 budget outlines and was passed by the House in December 2009 (H.R. 4154). Senate Democratic leaders supported the plan to enact the 2009 rules permanently (and make them retroactive to 2010). The Senate Republican leadership proposed a $5 million exemption and 35% rate. This latter provision was adopted for a two-year period, through 2012. At that point the exemption will revert to the pre-EGTRRA law. For estates of decedents in 2010, either the 2010 or 2011 rules can be elected. Spouses can inherit unused exemptions.

---

* This is an edited, reformatted and augmented version of a Congressional Research Service publication, CRS Report for Congress R41203, from www.crs.gov, dated December 23, 2010.

With any of the exemption levels, few estates are affected by the tax. In 2011, the shares of estates taxed are projected by one study to be 1.76%, 0.25%, and 0.14% for the exemption levels of $1 million, $3.5 million, and $5 million, respectively. These numbers would grow to 3%, 0.46%, and 0.23% by 2019. The revenue yield in 2011 is projected to be $34.4 billion, $18.2 billion, and $11.4 billion for the $1 million exemption/55% rate, $3.5 million exemption/45% rate, and the $5 million exemption/35% rate. The estate tax accounts for a small share of revenue.

The estate tax is a highly progressive tax; it not only applies to the largest estates, but within the distribution of estates a large share is concentrated in the over $20 million estate level: 72% for the $5 million/35% rate. Because of exclusions, the effective tax rates are smaller than the statutory rate, with an average of 14% for the $5 million exemption/35% rate. When distributed with respect to income, 96% falls in the top quintile of the income distribution, 72% in the top 1%, and 42% in the top 0.1%, under the $3.5 million exemption/45% rate.

Although concerns have been raised about the effects of the tax on small businesses and farmers, estimates indicate that the share of estate taxes paid by small business estates under the proposed revisions would be small (16% to 18%) and the share of estates of small business owners taxed is small (about 0.2% of decedents with at least 50% of their assets in businesses). Evidence suggests that the number of returns with inadequate liquid assets to pay the estate tax is negligible.

Other effects are likely small. The effects on savings are uncertain but likely small relative to the economy because the tax is small. Moving to either the $3.5 million plan or the $5 million plan would be projected to decrease charitable contributions by a small amount: 1% to 2%. Recent evidence suggests that the costs of administration and compliance are around 7% of revenues.

Structural reforms that might be considered are inheritance of spousal exemptions, and some reforms directed at abuses. A provision to restrict Grantor Retained Annuity Trusts (GRATS), which can be used to virtually eliminate estate tax by providing an annuity with a remainder, is contained in H.R. 4849. Other provisions in President Obama's budget outline include restricting discounts for estates left to family partnerships and conforming fair market value for purposes of the estate tax and future capital gains realizations for heirs.

INTRODUCTION

The Economic Growth and Tax Relief Act of 2001 (EGTRRA; P.L. 107-16), among other tax cuts, provided for a gradual reduction in the estate tax.

The estate tax applies to wealth transferred at death and had, at that time, a unified exemption for both lifetime gifts and the estate of $675,000.

Under EGTRRA, the estate tax exemption rose from $675,000 in 2001 to $3.5 million in 2009, and the top tax rate fell from 55% to 45%. Although combined estate and gift tax rates are graduated, the exemption is effectively in the form of a credit that eliminates tax due at lower rates so there is a flat rate on taxable assets under 2009 law. The gift tax exemption was, however, restricted to $1 million.

For 2010, EGTRRA scheduled the elimination of the estate tax, although it retained the gift tax and its $1 million exemption. EGTRRA also provided for a carryover of basis for assets inherited at death, so that, in contrast with prior law, heirs who sold assets would have to pay tax on gains accrued during the decedent's lifetime. This provision has a $1.3 million exemption for gain (plus $3 million for a spouse).

As with other provisions of EGTRRA, the tax revisions expire in 2011, returning the tax provisions to their pre-EGTRRA levels. The exemption would revert to $1 million (a value that had already been scheduled for pre-EGTRRA law) and the rate to 55% (with some graduated rates). The carryover basis provision effective in 2010 would be eliminated (so that heirs will not be taxed on gain accumulated during the decedent's life when they inherit assets).

During debate on the estate tax, most agreed that the 2010 provisions would not be continued, and, indeed, could be repealed retroactively. President Obama proposed a permanent extension of the 2009 rules (a $3.5 million exemption and a 45% tax rate), and the House provided for that permanent extension on December 3, 2009 (H.R. 4154). The Senate Democratic leadership has indicated a plan to retroactively reinstate the 2009 rules for 2010 and beyond. Senate Minority Leader McConnell proposed an alternative of a 35% tax rate and a $5 million exemption.[1] A similar proposal for a $5 million exemption and a 35% rate, which also includes the ability of the surviving spouse to inherit any unused exemption of the decedent, is often referred to as LincolnKyl after the two Senators who have supported it. Proposals have also been to begin with the $3.5 million/45% rate and phase in the $5 million/55% rate. Others have argued for a permanent estate tax repeal. [2] At the end of 2010, a temporary extension for two years, with a $5 million exemption, a 35% rate, and inheritance of unused spousal exemptions was enacted in P.L. 111- 312. At the end of 2012, absent legislation, the provisions will revert to the pre-EGTRRA rules ($1 million exemption, 55% top rate).

To address abuses and tax avoidance, President Obama has included proposals in his 2011 budget outline. One of these proposals, to reform the

Grantor Retained Annuity Trust (GRAT), is included in H.R. 4849. This provision is discussed in detail below.

After a brief description of the estate and gift tax and of options, this report compares the alternatives, focusing largely on a $1 million exemption and 55% rate, a $3.5 million exemption and a 45% rate, and a $5 million exemption and a 35% rate. Several policy effects and issues are analyzed: the share of decedents subject to tax; revenue effects; distributional effects; and effects on savings, charitable contributions, and compliance and administration. The report also considers other aspects of the proposals, such as whether the exemptions are indexed for inflation, a proposed inheritance of the exemption for spouses (which applies under the new rules to 2011 and 2012), and proposals to address perceived abuses.

Brief Description of the Estate Tax

This section describes the estate tax as it existed in 2009 and will exist in future years, absent legislative change. For 2010, there is no estate tax, although the gift tax remains and there is a tax on gains accumulated during the decedent's lifetime when assets are sold by heirs (with a $1.3 million exemption plus $3 million for a spouse). An election can be made for 2010 to apply either 2010 or 2011 rules. Because the exemption from gains is smaller than the overall estate tax exemption for 2011, some estates would have lower tax liability by electing the 2011 rules.

Basic Structure

The estate and gift tax is a unified tax, so that assets transferred as gifts during a person's lifetime are combined with those transferred at death (bequests) and subject to a single rate schedule.[3] The tax is imposed on the decedent's estate and the rate structure applies to total bequests and gifts given; heirs are not subject to tax. In the past, a single effective exemption applied, but under the 2001 tax revisions effective in 2009, the gift tax exemption was more limited than the combined exemption for both estate and gift taxes. Thus, although a unified rate schedule applies to both bequests and gifts, the exemptions differed in 2009. The combined exemption was $3.5 million, whereas the exemption for gifts was $1 million. For 2011 and 2012, the combined exemption is $5 million and that exemption applies to gifts as well. In 2013, the combined exemption will be $1 million, absent legislative change.

Although the rates of the tax are graduated, the exemption is applied in the form of a credit and offsets taxes applied at the lower rates, under the 2009 and the 2011-2012 rules. Thus the taxable estate was subject to a flat 45% rate in 2009 and will be subject to a flat 35% rate in 2011-2012. Under pre-EGTRRA law, which will apply in 2013, absent legislation, there are some graduated rates on taxable estate amounts between $1 million and $3 million because the exemption is not large enough to offset tax at lower rates. Rates begin at 41% for amounts over $1 million and rise by 2 percentage points at each additional $500,000, reaching 53% on amounts between $2.5 million and $3 million. There is also a 5% surtax designed to phase out the benefits of lower rates so that very large estates are taxed at a flat 55% rate. Individuals are also allowed to exempt annual gifts of $13,000 per recipient, which are not counted as part of the lifetime exemption. The annual gift tax exemption is indexed for inflation in $1,000 increments. A generation skipping tax is also imposed, to address estate tax avoidance through gifts and bequests to a later generation.[4]

Exemptions and Deductions

Estates are allowed to exempt some assets from the estate tax and take a deduction for selected other transfers. Transfers between spouses are exempt. Estates are also allowed to take deductions for charitable contributions and administrative expenses. Currently estates are also allowed a deduction for taxes paid on estates and inheritances imposed by states. Prior to 2001, a credit was allowed, subject to a cap, for state estate taxes, but the credit was phased out and replaced by a deduction in that legislation. (Should EGTRRA provisions expire, the state credit would reappear.)

Under the rules for 2011 and 2012, a spouse can inherit any unused exemption. Thus if a husband dies and leaves an estate of $3 million, the remainder of his $5 million exemption can be used by his wife, whose exemption would be increased by the $2 million difference.

Special Provisions for Small Businesses, Farms, and Landowners

A series of provisions benefit small businesses, including farms or landowners. These include the ability of family businesses to pay the tax in installments with only interest payments during part of the installment period, special use valuation, conservation easements, and, if the law reverts to its 2001 rules, a deduction for family owned business assets. Minority discounts, although granted by courts rather than specifically in the law, may also benefit small businesses.

Although the estate tax return is due within nine months of the death, small businesses are allowed to defer payment (except for interest) for the next five years, and pay the remaining installment payments over 10 years. Since the last interest payment and the first installment coincide, the overall delay in full payment is 14 years. The benefit is allowed only for the business portion of assets and only if 35% of the estate is in a farm or closely held business.

Small businesses are also allowed to value their assets at use as a farm or business. This provision is particularly beneficial to farms and allows a reduction in the estate value of up to $1 million. It means, for example, that the value of the farm will be what it could be sold for if restricted to farm use rather than, for example, to be subdivided for development. Heirs are required to continue use as a farm or business for 10 years.

Farmers and other landowners may also benefit from conservation easements, a perpetual restriction on the use of the land where, in addition to the reduction in value due to the easement itself, an exclusion of up to 40% of the restricted value of the land, capped at $500,000, is allowed.

In prior law, another provision benefitting small businesses was the Qualified Family Owned Business Income (QFOBI) deduction. This provision allowed estates with at least half of their assets in a family business to take a deduction for these business assets. This provision originally allowed up to $675,000 of business deductions at a time when the basic estate tax exemption was $625,000, and imposed an overall cap of $1.3 million on the total of both deductions. Once the regular exemption passed the $1.3 million level, the provision was no longer relevant. If the 2001 tax cuts sunset in 2013, the exemption will become $1 million and QFOBI will be relevant again, allowing an additional $300,000 exemption. With the $5 million exemption for 2011 and 2012, this provision is ineffective. To qualify for the QFOBI deduction, heirs must continue the business for 10 years or the tax saving must be repaid.

Step up in Basis for Appreciated Assets

Heirs take as their basis (the amount to be deducted from the sales price) for purposes of future capital gains the value of the asset at the date of the decedent's death. This treatment is referred to as step-up in basis and means that no capital gains tax is paid on the appreciation of assets during the decedent's lifetime. For example, if decedent purchased stock for $100,000 and the value of the stock at the time of death is $200,000, if the heir sells the property for $250,000 a gain of $50,000 ($250,000 minus the stepped-up basis of $200,000) is recognized. The $100,000 of gain that accrued during the decedent's lifetime is never taxed. The step up rules do not apply to gifts, where carryover basis is applied. In that case, the original basis of $100,000 would be carried over and the gain would be $150,000 ($250,000 minus $100,000). Both the gain accrued by the donor and the gain accrued by the donee are taxed. The step-up rules do not apply to bequests for 2010, if 2010 rules are elected, where carryover basis, with an exemption, applies, as noted above.

Differences in the Treatment of Bequests and Gifts

Aside from the different exemption levels in some estate tax rules, there are other differences between the taxation of gifts and bequests. As noted above, gifts do not benefit from the step up in basis. The donor takes the basis in the hands of the donor, generally the original cost of acquiring the assets. The basis cannot be less than the fair market value at the time of the gift if a loss is realized.

At the same time, the gift tax is tax exclusive (the tax is imposed on the gift net of the tax) whereas the estate tax is tax inclusive (the tax is applied to the estate inclusive of the tax). To illustrate, consider a 50% tax rate. Assuming the exemption is already used, to provide a gift of $1 million costs $1.5 million: the tax rate of 50% is applied to the gift of $1 million for a $0.5 million tax. To provide a net amount of $1 million for a bequest, $2 million is required: a tax of $1 million (50% of $2 million) and a net to the heir of $1 million. Another way of stating this is that the gift tax rate, if stated as a tax inclusive rate like the estate tax, would be 33%. Thus for the 55%, 45%, and 35% estate tax rates, the gift tax rate equivalents are 35%, 31%, and 26%.[5]

OPTIONS FOR REVISION

The principal components of any policy that continues the estate tax are the amount of the exemption and the tax rate.[6] As indicated earlier, the exemption in 2009 was $3.5 million, the exemption is scheduled at $5 million for 2011 and 2012, and in 2013 the estate tax will revert to an exemption of $1 million, absent a change in the statute. Thus, while any level of exemption might be considered, the two most common levels mentioned are $3.5 million and $5 million. The level of the exemption affects not only the revenue but the number of estates that are subject to the tax.

The second principal component of a continued estate tax is the rate, which will return to 55% in 2013 absent legislative change; rates of 45% applied in 2009 and a 35% rate applies in 2011- 2012. Some proposals would apply the capital gains tax rate (currently 15% but scheduled to go to 20% in 2013) or some multiple of it.

Another issue is whether to index the exemption for inflation. Some components of the income tax, such as rate brackets and standard deductions, are indexed, while others (such as child credits) are not. Over time, as prices rise, a fixed exemption causes more estates to be subject to tax. Without indexation, Congress may return from time to time to reconsider the exemption.

A final issue is the potential carryforward of an unused estate tax exemption to the surviving spouse. The provision, adopted in recent legislation for 2011 and 2012, would allow spouses to inherit unused estate tax exemptions. Since bequests to the spouse are excluded from the estate, the couple together can have a larger total exemption if the first spouse to die leaves assets to the children or other heirs large enough to absorb his or her estate exemption. This action will reduce the size of the estate subject to tax when the second spouse dies. There are reasons, however, that the taxpayer may prefer to leave more assets to a spouse (for example, if there are concerns about having enough assets to live in comfort or cover emergencies). The proposed change is to permit the second spouse to inherit any unused exemption and add it to his or her own future exemption.

Proposals have also been made to increase the percentage or dollar limits of special use valuations and conservation easements. At the same time, there are proposals, including those in President Obama's budget, to restrict practices considered as abuses. One proposal, relating to a certain type of trust (a Grantor Retained Annuity Trust or GRAT) was adopted in H.R. 4849, the Small Business and Infrastructure Jobs Tax Act of 2010. Another proposal would restrict minority discounts for estates that are sometimes allowed by courts when no one heir has a controlling interest in the property. A third provision would require estates and heirs use the same fair market value in determining the valuation for purposes of the estate tax and for determining basis in the hands of the heir.

An Introduction to the Issues

Data, other empirical evidence, and economic theory can help address proposals to revise the estate tax. Relevant economic issues include the scope and effect of the tax on the total population and the distribution of the tax, the revenue yield, and the potential effects on family businesses, savings, administration and compliance, and charitable giving. To the extent possible, different options are compared in the context of these issues.

Other issues are perhaps more philosophical or, as Gale and Slemrod discuss in their article on the estate tax, rhetorical.[7] For example, some people oppose the estate tax because they hold a philosophical view that the estate tax is a death tax and death should not be taxed. Arguments are also made that estate taxes result in a double tax, because assets have already been taxed under the income tax and should not be taxed again. Gale and Slemrod do point out, however, the complexity of the rhetorical questions. For example, they point out that for the vast majority of people (at the time they were writing, 98%) death actually brings potential tax benefits through the forgiveness of tax on accrued but unrealized gains (gains on assets that have not been sold). They also note that income from unrealized appreciation in assets is not taxed during the lifetime and so is not subject to double taxation. They indicate that 36% of estate assets and 80% of the wealth in closely held business and farm estates is from unrealized appreciation.

Supporters of the estate tax may believe it is important to constrain the accumulation of wealth generation after generation. While empirical evidence can demonstrate that the estate tax is highly progressive, the degree to which taxes should be applied to large amounts of wealth in pursuit of reducing inequality in society, much like the question of whether it is wrong for death to trigger a tax, is a value judgment.

Coverage of Decedents

The estate tax has never affected more than a small fraction of decedents. Table 1 indicates that if the law reverts to the $1 million exemption, less than 2% of decedents would pay an estate tax. Table 1 also indicates that restoring the $3.5 million exemption leads to a quarter of 1% of decedents paying the tax. Moving to a $5 million exemption reduces the share to 0.14%. The column for 2019 illustrates the effects of indexing the $3.5 million and the $5 million for inflation, starting from 2009. Note that even with indexing for inflation, real asset growth leads to an increased share of decedents paying the estate tax. With or without indexing, the $3.5 million option will affect less than one-half of 1% of decedents and the $5 million option will affect less than one-fourth of 1% of decedents. If the main focus of legislation is to exclude all but a small fraction of estates from the tax, the $3.5 million exemption and the $5 million exemption accomplish that goal, and indexing does not matter very much over short time horizons.

Table 1. Percentage of Decedents Subject to Estate Tax

Exemption Level	2011	2019
$ 1 million	1.76	3.00
$3.5 million	0.25	0.46
$3.5 million, indexed for inflation	0.24	0.32
$5 million	0.14	0.23
$5 million, indexed for inflation	0.14	0.18

Source: Based on data in Urban Brookings Tax Policy Center, Table T09-0431, http://www.taxpolicycenter.org/numbers/displayatab.cfm?DocID=2506&topic2ID=60&topic3ID=66&DocTypeID=.

Note: For proposals that are indexed, the indexation begins from 2009.

Liabilities and Revenue Loss

An issue in the choice of estate tax provisions is the revenue cost. Although the estate tax accounts for a small share of total federal revenues, 1.3% in 2012 if the $1 million exemption/55% rate provisions are retained, concerns remain about revenue losses.

Revenue costs are normally estimated against a current law baseline. Thus, the cost of keeping the 2009 rules in place retroactively to 2010, with a $3.5 million exemption and a 45% tax rate, would be compared to no estate tax in 2010; therefore there would be a revenue gain compared to no estate tax. In subsequent years, where current law reverts to a larger estate tax (a $1 million exemption and 55% rate) the smaller estate tax will lead to a revenue loss. Receipts are also measured when they flow into the Treasury and there is a delay in the filing of estate tax returns. The Joint Committee on Taxation (JCT) in 2009 estimated a gain of $0.5 billion in FY2010, then a loss, rising to $38 billion in FY2019 for a total of $234 billion over the 10-year period (FY2010-FY2019) from retaining the 2009 exemptions. Treasury's estimates are smaller, with a $3 billion and a $1 billion gain respectively in the first two fiscal years, becoming a $28 billion loss by FY2019, and losing $171 billion over a 10-year period.[8]

Another way to examine the alternatives is to look at the estimated yield for alternative proposals, that is, the liability rather than the flow of revenue to the Treasury. Table 2 provides data from the Urban Brookings Tax Policy Center for the three exemption levels. In 2011, the scheduled rules ($1 million exemption, 55% rate) are estimated to produce a liability of $34.4 billion; the $3.5 million exemption, 45% rate a revenue of $18.2 billion, and the $5 million exemption/35% rate a revenue of $11.4 billion. Thus, in 2010, the reduced liability from moving to a $3.5 million exemption with a 45% rate is $16.3 billion, whereas moving to the $5 million exemption with a 45% rate loses an additional $6.9 billion, for a total of $26.2 billion. The cost increases over time as the real and nominal value of wealth grows, so that, for example, the reduction in tax from moving to a $3.5 million exemption and 45% rate increases from $16.3 billion in 2011 to $30.7 billion in 2019.

Table 2. Estate Tax Liability under Alternative Proposals ($billions)

Exemption Level/Rate	2011	2019
$ 1 million, 55% rate	34.4	62.2
$3.5 million/45% rate	18.1	31.5
$3.5 million, indexed for inflation/ 45% rate	17.9	28.9
$5 million/ 35% rate	11.2	20.9
$5 million, indexed for inflation/ 35% rate	11.2	17.9

Source: Based on data in Urban Brookings Tax Policy Center, Table T09-0431, http://www.taxpolicycenter.org/ numbers/displayatab.cfm?DocID=2506&topic2ID=60&topic3ID=66&DocTypeID=. Note that numbers are slightly different from those in Table 3 due to an earlier estimation date.

Notes: For proposals that are indexed, indexation begins from 2009.

Table 2 also contains estimates of estate tax liability if exemptions are indexed (assuming indexing back to 2009). Indexing does not make a great deal of difference over this time period. Real growth in wealth is more important. For example the difference between revenues in 2011 and 2019 for the $3.5 million exemption/45% rate is $13.4 billion but only $2.6 billion of the difference is due to lack of indexing for inflation.

The estimates in Table 2 indicate that the difference between the $1 million, 55% rate and the $5 million, 35% rate would be $23.2 billion ($34.4 minus $11.2), in turn suggesting a cost for two years of $46 billion. The Joint Committee on Taxation (JCT) has estimated the cost of the estate tax revisions at $68 billion. Some of this difference may reflect differences in data and projections, but the JCT estimates would also be increased because of the increase in the gift tax exemption and the ability to inherit exemptions. For example, if a husband or wife left all assets to his or her spouse, the maximum exemption of the second spouse would be larger by $5 million.

As indicated above, the two proposals generally discussed during the 111th Congress were the $3.5 million exemption and 45% tax rate, and the $5 million exemption and 35% tax rate. However, various combinations of rates and exemptions could be considered. Table 3 reports the estimates of estate tax liability for each of the three exemption levels at different rates. It shows that, compared with the default $1 million exemption, a larger amount of the revenue loss results from moving to the $3.5 million exemption rather than the 45% rate. Similarly, in moving from the $1 million to the $5 million exemption, the cost of the exemption increase is smaller than lowering the rate to 35%. However, once the exemption is set a $3.5 million and the rate at 45%, the cost of moving to a $5 million exemption ($14.2 billion) is about the same as the cost of moving to a 35% tax rate ($14.1 billion).

The rate reductions tend to benefit, relatively, a wealthier group of estates than exemptions, and thus reduce progressivity of the estate tax. However, rate reductions also reduce the average marginal tax rate more than exemption increases, which could matter for economic efficiency. These distributional issues are discussed more fully in the next section.

Table 3. Estate Tax Liability 2011: Exemption and Rate ($billions)

Exemption Level	55% rate	45% rate	35% rate
$1 million	34.4	28.1	21.8
$3.5 million	22.1	18.1	14.1
$5 million	17.4	14.2	11.2

Source: Based on data in Urban Brookings Tax Policy Center, Table T10-0269, http://www.taxpolicycenter.org/numbers/displayatab.cfm?Docid=2868&DocTypeID=7.

Note: The revenue effect for lower rates under the $1 million exemption is somewhat overstated because of the lower graduated rates.

Distributional Issues

One of the rationales for an estate tax is to impose a tax on high income and high wealth taxpayers, and contribute to the progressivity of the tax system. As indicated in the discussion of coverage, all of the proposals fall on a small proportion of decedents and thus, due to the size of the exemption level, on those with the greatest wealth. The alternative proposals have different effects on the size of estates covered and the distribution of taxes.

As indicated in Table 4, the number of estates is concentrated in the smaller estates. With the $1 million exemption, about half of the estates subject to tax have assets of under $2 million and almost 80% have assets of under $3.5 million and these estates would be eliminated from estate tax coverage with either the $3.5 million or the $5 million exemption. With a $3.5 million exemption, the share of taxable estates under $5 million is smaller than the share falling between $5 million to $10 million group. Of the returns taxed under the $3.5 million exclusion, 23% are less than $5 million in assets and would not be taxed under the $5 million exclusion.

Table 4. Percentage Distribution of Taxable Estate Tax Returns by Size of Estate, 2011

Size of Estate ($millions)	$1 Million Exemption, 55% Rate (43,540 returns)	$3.5 Million Exemption, 45% Rate (6,46 returns)	$5 Million Exemption, 35% Rate (3,600 returns)
1-2	49.8	0.0	0.0
2-3.5	27.5	0.0	0.0
3.5-5	9.2	21.87	0.0
5-10	8.1	45.5	43.9
10-20	3.1	19.8	33.3
Over 20	2.3	12.8	22.8
Total	100.0	100.0	100.0

Source: Based on data in Urban Brookings Tax Policy Center, Tables T10-0269, http://www.taxpolicycenter.org/numbers/displayatab.cfm?Docid=2868&DocTypeID=7.

Table 5. Percentage Distribution of Estate Tax Revenue by Type of Return, 2011

Size of Estate ($millions)	$1 Million Exemption, 55% Rate ($34.4 billion total)	$3.5 Million Exemption, 45% Rate ($18.2 billion total)	$5 Million Exemption, 35% Rate ($11.4 billion total)
1-2	6.9	0.0	0.0
2-3.5	15.8	0.0	0.0
3.5-5	10.3	1.9	0.0
5-10	18.5	15.7	9.2
10-20	14.5	20.0	18.6
Over 20	34.0	62.4	72.2
Total	100.0	100.0	100.0

Source: Based on data in Urban Brookings Tax Policy Center, Tables T10-0269, http://www.taxpolicycenter.org/numbers/displayatab.cfm?Docid=2868&DocTypeID=7.

As shown in Table 5, revenue from the estate tax is more concentrated in larger estates. The largest share of revenue is in the $20 million and above class regardless of the exemption. With a return to the $1 million exemption that class would pay one-third of the revenue; with a $3.5 million exemption it would pay over 60% and with a $5 million exemption it would pay almost three-quarters of the estate tax. These estimates indicate that the estate tax not only applies to high wealth families, but with either the $3.5 million or the $5 million exemption more than half the revenue is collected from estates with $20 million or more in assets.

Although the statutory marginal tax rates are often criticized as being very high, the average share of the estate paid in tax is much lower. Part of the reason for the lower effective tax rate is the exemption. For example, even if a $10 million estate has no other deductions and exemption, a $3.5 million exemption means only $6.5 million is taxed. The tax of $2.95 million (45% of $6.5 million) is a tax of 29.5% on the $10 million.

As shown in Table 6, the effective tax averages less than 20% for estates up to $20 million and the average rate on those estates is less than 20%. The effective tax rate also rises, generally, with estate size, which would be expected as the exemption is a smaller share of the estate. With the $1 million exemption, the tax is 16.5% in the highest class, while it is 16% under the $3.5 million exemption and 11.5% under the $5 million exemptions. Important reasons for lower effective tax rates are the exemption, spousal transfers, and charitable contributions. The decline in effective tax rate at the very highest estate size for the $1 million exemption may reflect the greater likelihood of charitable contributions and the lesser importance of the exemption.

Table 6. Effective Estate Tax Rate (Tax as Percentage of Assets), 2011

Size of Estate ($millions)	$1 Million Exemption, 55% Rate	$3.5 Million Exemption, 45% Rate	$5 Million Exemption, 35% Rate
1-2	7.3	0.0	0.0
2-3.5	17.7	0.0	0.0
3.5-5	21.4	5.9	0.0
5-10	26.3	13.9	8.7
10-20	28.3	21.5	13.2
Over 20	19.4	21.6	16.1

Source: Based on data in Urban Brookings Tax Policy Center, Table T10-0269, http://www.taxpolicycenter.org/numbers/displayatab.cfm?Docid=2868&DocTypeID=7.

Most distributional analyses of taxes are reported relative to income. As shown in Table 7, the Tax Policy Center has estimated the distribution by income class of the tax for the $1 million exemption /55% rate and the $3.5 million exemption/45% tax rate. As this table indicates, the estate tax is highly concentrated in the higher income classes. For the $1 million exemption, 83% of the tax falls in the top quintile and 45% of the tax in the top 1%. For the $3.5 million exemption, 96% of the tax is imposed on the top quintile and 72% on the top 1%. These results indicate that the estate tax is a highly progressive feature of the federal tax system.[9]

Table 7. Distribution of Estate Taxes by Income Class

Income Share	$1 Million Exemption, 55% Rate	$3.5 Million Exemption, 45% Rate
Bottom Quintile	0.3	0.1
Second Quintile	0.9	0.2
Middle Quintile	5.2	0.4
Fourth Quintile	8.9	0.4
Top Quintile	83.1	96.2
80-90th Percentile	8.6	2.0
90-95th Percentile	6.0	1.3
95-99th Percentile	23.4	20.8
Top 1%	45.0	72.0
Top 0.1%	22.6	42.1

Source: Based on data from Urban Brookings Tax Policy Center, Tables T10-0073 and T09-0402, http://www.taxpolicycenter.org/numbers/displayatab.cfm?DocID=2664&topic2ID=60&topic3ID=66&DocTypeID= .

Notes: Distribution for the $1 million exemption is based on combined data with distributions for 2009 and 2012, weighted by 2010 revenue effects. Distribution for the $3.5 million exemption is for 2009.

Effects on Small Businesses and Farmers

An issue that has played an important role in the debate over the estate tax is the possible impact on small businesses and farms. The role played by the small business issue in the original 2001 legislation is detailed by Graetz and Shapiro.[10] Arguments were made that the estate tax causes families to have to sell businesses to pay the estate tax because there are not enough liquid assets to pay the tax.

According to aggregate data for 2008, farm assets account for 2.4% of assets reported on estate tax returns, and business assets constitute 17.9%.[11] These shares include assets of estates where business or farm assets may be a minor part of the estate.

Table 8. Coverage of Estates with At Least Half of Assets in a Business, 2011

Exemption	Taxable Estate Returns	Percentage of all Taxable Estate Returns	Estimated Taxable Estates of Businesses as a Percentage of Decedents with Business Assets
$1 million	2980	6.8	1.6
$3.5 million	520	8.0	0.2
$5 million	440	9.7	0.2

Source: Based on data from Urban Brookings Tax Policy Center. Columns (2) and (3) from Table T10-0269. http://www.taxpolicycenter.org/numbers/displayatab.cfm?Docid=2868&DocTypeID=7. For final column, data on Taxable Estates of with Half of More of the Estate in Business Assets from Tables T09-0196, T09-0i98, and T09- 0199, http://www.taxpolicycenter.org/numbers/displayatab.cfm?DocID=2270&topic2ID=60&topic3ID=66& DocTypeID=. Data on total number of estates and total decedents from Table T09-0431, http://www.taxpolicycenter.org/numbers/displayatab.cfm?DocID=2506&topic2ID=60&topic3ID=66&DocTypeID= . Data on the share of tax returns with at least half of income from business is from Table T09-0426, http://www.taxpolicycenter.org/numbers/displayatab.cfm?DocID=2501&topic2ID=60&topic3ID=73&DocTypeID= .

Notes: To estimate the share of decedents with business assets, the share of income tax returns with more than half of income from small business (7.5%) was multiplied by the total number of decedents.

Evidence on the effect of the tax on small business suggests that the taxable business estates are a small share of all taxable estates and a small share of estates of all business decedents. Table 8 provides estimates for the coverage of the estate tax reported or derived from the Urban Brookings Tax

Policy Center of estates with at least half of their assets in business. As shown in the table, these estates are less than 10% of taxable estates, and, as with other estates, only a small fraction of business estates pay the estate tax (0.2% for the $3.5 million and $5 million exemption).

As shown in Table 9, data indicate that returns with business assets account for a somewhat higher share of the estate tax than they do of the number of taxable estates, suggesting some larger concentration of business assets in larger estates. (Note that in this case, the tax paid reflects total estate tax, and thus includes tax on business and non-business assets.) However, the effective tax rates (taxes paid as a percentage of the assets of all estates of $1 million or more) are somewhat lower for these small business returns, suggesting the use of discounts may be important.

Table 9. Taxes Paid on Small Business Estates, 2011

Exemption/Rate	Estate Tax Liability ($billions)	Share of Estate Tax Liability	Effective Tax Rate, Business Estates	Effective Tax Rates, All Estates
$1 million, 55%	3.9	11.4	16.8	18.9
$3.5 million, 45%	2.9	16.1	18.1	18.9
$5 million, 35%	2.0	17.8	13.3	14.4

Source: Based on data from Urban Brookings Tax Policy Center Table T10-0269, http://www.taxpolicycenter.org/numbers/displayatab.cfm?Docid=2868&DocTypeID=7.

Although the Urban Brookings Tax Policy Center did not separately estimate farmer estates or consider questions of whether these estates had adequate liquid assets to pay the tax, a study done by the Congressional Budget Office (CBO) did examine these issues. This CBO study likely defined farmers more broadly than the Tax Policy Center criterion. At the same time, it examined the subset of estates that took the QFOBI exemption, which would be both small business and farm estates where the heirs expected to continue the business and where more than half of the estate was in the family business. The analysis was for 2000. Column 2 of Table 10 reports those values at an average annual growth rate of 3.5% for 11 years (for 2000 to 2011), to project the Effective Tax Rates, All Estates distribution across estate sizes for 2011. (This measure increases the value by the average annual growth rate of the economy minus growth in the labor force for 2000-2009, applied over 11 years, thus taking into account real wealth growth as well as inflation.)

Table 10 indicates that the number of farm estates, using their measure of farms subject to the tax, would be less than 123 estates at the $3.5 million exemption and about 65 at the $5 million exemption. These estates are about 2% of all estates owing tax. The number of returns claiming QFOBI are also small, accounting for 2% to 2.5% of all taxable estate returns.

Table 10. Number of Farm Estates or Estates Claiming QFOBI Deductions with Estate Tax Liability at Different Exemption Levels

2000 Exemption Level ($millions)	Level Adjusted for 2011 ($ millions)	Number of Farm Estates	Percentage of Total Estates	Number of QFOBI Estates	Percentage of Total Estates
0.675	1.0	1659	3.2	485	0.9
1.5	2.2	300	2.2	223	1.6
2.0	3.0	123	1.9	135	2.1
3.5	5.1	65	1.8	94	2.5

Source: Congressional Budget Office, *Effects of the Federal Estate Tax on Farms and Small Businesses*, July 2005. http://www.cbo.gov/ftpdocs/65xx/doc6512/07-06-EstateTax.pdf.

Table 11 shows results the study found for a second question: how many estates of these types are likely to have insufficient liquid assets in the estate to pay the tax liability? While there were 138 farm estates in these circumstances for the $1 million exemption, there were only about 15 for the larger exemptions. These returns account for 0.2% and 0.4% of returns paying estate tax. For estates claiming the QFOBI deduction there were 62 at the $3.5 million exemption and 41 at the $5 million exemption. These returns accounted for about 1% of taxable estates.

A different survey of farmers performed by the Department of Agriculture estimated that farm estates would pay $683 million in estate taxes in 2009, which would be just under 4% of total estate tax liability, and that 1.6% of farms decedents would pay the estate tax under the 2009 provisions.[12]

This share is much larger than the share for businesses overall reported by the Tax Policy Center and is also about twice as large as the estimates implied by the CBO study.[13]

Table 11. Number of Farm Estates or Estates Claiming QFOBI with Insufficient Liquid Assets to Pay the Tax

2000 Exemption ($millions)	Level Adjusted for 2011 ($millions)	Number of Farm Estates with Insufficient Liquidity	Percentage of Total Estates	Number of QFOBI Estates with Insufficient Liquidity	Percentage of Total Estates
0.675	1.0	138	0.3	164	0.3
1.5	2.2	27	0.2	82	0.5
2.0	3.0	15	0.2	62	0.9
3.5	5.1	13	0.4	41	1.1

Source: Congressional Budget Office, Effects of the Federal Estate Tax on Farms and Small Businesses, July 2005, http://www.cbo.gov/ftpdocs/65xx/doc6512/07-06-EstateTax.pdf.

Regardless of the data source used, the evidence suggests two important characteristics of businesses and the estate tax: businesses pay a small fraction of the estate tax and a tiny fraction of total estates of businesses and farmers are liable for the tax. If estate tax policy decisions are driven by these concerns, a more target-efficient alternative would be to provide additional benefits for business assets, such as an expanded QFOBI deduction.[14]

Effects on Savings and Output

Some claims have been made that the estate tax causes a significant reduction in savings. This effect may be alleged to be so damaging that it justifies eliminating the tax. However, there is no clear basis for this claim. Economic theory does not provide a clear guide. If the bequest motive is primarily to leave a bequest to one's heirs because of concerns about their welfare, the estate tax could lead to less saving (because a gift to one's children is made more costly relative to one's own consumption, the substitution effect), or it could lead to more savings to retain a larger amount after the estate tax is paid (the income effect). These offsetting income and substitution effects create an ambiguous theoretical prediction about the effect of the estate tax on savings. If the main purpose of accumulating assets is to provide a precautionary savings amount (to account for catastrophic illness, for example), the estate tax does not matter, since it is irrelevant to that purpose.

With theoretical uncertainty, the issue becomes an empirical one. Here, however, there is virtually no empirical evidence. In the single study of the wealth elasticity of estates (the percentage change in wealth divided by the percentage change in taxes), Kopczuk and Slemrod characterized their results as fragile, meaning that the results depended on model specification.[15]

A study by Holtz-Eakin and Smith used an elasticity from one of the specifications in the Kopczuk and Slemrod study to estimate that the estate tax caused a decrease in wealth of $1.6 trillion.[16] Although this estimate was based on total projected wealth associated with those filing estate tax returns (in 2004), the report indicated the increase in capital was an increase in small business capital (although, as noted above small businesses account for only a fraction, about 16%, of the estate tax). That estimate was, in turn, used to project increases in hiring by small businesses.

The effect projected in the Holtz-Eakin and Smith study appears quite large.[17] As a simple illustration, consider that the effect of estate taxes on savings should be similar to the effect of capital income taxes in general. In 2007, the last year for which data on sources of income in the income tax were available, the estate tax accounted for only 4% of capital income tax revenue at the Federal level.[18] This ratio implies that eliminating capital income taxes would increase wealth by $40 trillion ($1.6 trillion dividend by 0.04). This amount would be an approximate doubling of the total U.S. capital stock.[19] Even the most generous model with infinitely elastic savings responses tends to produce an increase of about one-third that size, and estimates based on the higher end of empirically estimated time-series savings rates would suggest a result only one-tenth of that size. Some effects from dynamic models, depending on how the revenue loss is offset, are negative or negligible.[20]

One problem with the estimate in the estate tax study is that it did not take account of feedback effects from the economy, particularly the decline in pre-tax return when the capital stock expands.[21] That feedback effect is the reason that an infinitely elastic response leads to a limited effect: the capital stock expands only enough to drive the after tax return back to its original value.

Given lack of theoretical and empirical evidence it is not possible to precisely determine what the effect of repealing the estate tax on savings, but it is likely to be small, simply because the yield of the tax is small. Any effect on the stock of capital in small business should only be a fraction of that amount.

The tax rate is more important than the exemption in determining any positive effects of reducing the estate tax on savings, since that rate is more important for the marginal rate that drives the substitution effect. Exemptions affect the substitution effect by pushing some income into a zero marginal tax rate, but are more important for the average rates that determine the income effect, so that higher exemptions are less likely to increase savings than higher rates.

Effect on Charitable Contributions

Unlike the effect of the estate tax on savings, there is an extensive empirical literature on the response of charitable bequests in the estate tax, and the evidence indicates a significant response of bequests. Nevertheless, according to a recent CRS study, the effect on overall charitable giving is likely to be small: moving from the $1 million exemption with a 55% tax rate to the $3.5 million exemption with a 45% tax rate would be projected to lower charitable giving by 1%; moving to the $5 million exemption with a 35% rate would be projected to reduce giving by 2%.[22] These relatively small effects occur largely because only 4% to 6% of giving is affected by the estate tax. The effects would be larger for foundations and certain types of organizations (such as higher education) that are more likely to receive bequests.

Administrative and Compliance Cost

Another issue is the degree to which the estate tax causes excessive compliance and planning costs for taxpayers, and administrative costs for the IRS. Some arguments have been made that these costs, particularly for estate planning, are as large as the estate tax itself. Gale and Slemrod, however, review the limited evidence and conclude that the cost of administration and compliance is probably in the neighborhood of 7% of revenues, with almost all of that cost due to planning and compliance.[23]

Other Design Issues

This section briefly discusses proposals to revise certain features of the estate tax. These include portability of the spousal exemption, changing the rules on certain trusts, restricting minority discounts, and conforming definitions of fair market value for estates and heirs.[24]

Portability of the Spousal Exemption

Because transfers between spouses are exempt from the estate tax, the estate exemption is of no value to a person who transfers all of his or her estate to a spouse. For example, if the estate tax exemption is $3.5 million and a couple jointly owns assets of $8 million ($4 million each), if the first spouse to die leaves $4 million to the second spouse, and the second spouse then leaves $8 million to children, $4.5 million of the estate will be subject to tax. If the first spouse to die left $3.5 million to the children directly, then the second spouse would have an estate of $4.5 million, with only $1 million subject to the estate tax.

There are estate planning options (such as credit shelter trusts) that can address this issue. However, these options (which may also require an initial transfer of assets between spouses) not only require complicated estate tax planning but also may cause taxpayers to dispose of their assets in a way that they would not prefer.

Simply allowing a spouse to inherit any unused portion of the exemption is an alternative. In the example above, all of the assets could be left to the remaining spouse on the death of the first spouse, and the second spouse to die would be able to claim a total exemption of $7 million (the sum of both exemptions). Portability can also be valuable with assets, such as pension rights, that cannot be transferred. This portability feature has been adopted for the extension of the estate tax for 2011 and 2012.

Although there are some advantages to this provision in both equity and simplified planning, there are problems as well. First, the portability provision, if made permanent, will cost increasing amounts of revenue in the future. The JCT provided estimates suggesting that the number of estates benefitting from portability will increase by 14 times over 10 years.[25] Thus, allowing portability is likely to substantially decrease revenues in the long run. However, it may be more likely to benefit smaller estates where it may be more difficult to engage in the types of transfers and planning needed to absorb the credits.

There are some complications as well for designing and administering this provision, some of which are detailed in the JCT study.[26] Second (and more) marriages raise an issue. Should the inheritance be allowed for future marriages or should it be inherited only once? That is, suppose a widow remarries, and then dies leaving all her assets to a second spouse: does the second spouse inherit two exemptions or one? Is there a possibility for deathbed marriages to terminally ill low income individuals to generate an additional deduction (and how can that be distinguished from "legitimate" marriages with a tragic early death)?

The 2011 provision allows multiple inheritances but limits the exclusion to the last predeceased spouse, which affects total exclusions available in second marriages depending on the order of death. Thus if a wife's husband number two dies first, she gets the smaller of the exemptions from husband one and husband two, whereas if the wife dies first, husband number two gets all unused exemptions, whether they are his wife's own exemptions or inherited from husband number one.

Another question is: should the value of the inherited exemption be limited to the value of the spouse's estate? That seems to be a reasonable rule. Otherwise, if the second spouse continues to accumulate wealth, the portability would effectively increase the exemption over the amount available had each spouse absorbed the exemption in their own estate. Such a rule, however, would require the filing of estate tax returns and valuation of the estate when they would not otherwise be subject to tax. There would also be issues about how to reconstruct fair market value, if the portability were allowed if the first estate tax return were not filed. As with many solutions that seem simple, complications remain. The 2011 -2012 provision allows the exemption to exceed the value of the estate, but requires a declaration be made on the estate return for the exemption to be transferred. Thus, presumably those who do not file an estate return because they are below the filing threshold or otherwise make a declaration will not benefit from the portability rule.

Grantor Retained Annuity Trusts

A Grantor Retained Annuity Trust (GRAT) is a trust that allows the grantor to receive an annuity, with any remaining assets transferred to the trust recipient. The value of the gift is reduced by the value of the assets used to fund the annuity. If the assets in the trust appreciate substantially, then virtually all of the gift can be reduced by the value of the annuity, while still providing a substantial ultimate gift to the recipient. If the grantor dies during the annuity period the remaining value of the annuity is included in the estate. Thus for this trust approach to be a method of transferring assets roughly tax free, the assets must appreciate at a rate faster than the discount rate used to value the annuity, and the grantor needs to survive over the period of the annuity. To assure the latter will be likely to occur, many of these trusts have very short annuity periods, as short as two years. The GRAT proposal contained in H.R. 4849 and in the President's budget proposals[27] would impose a minimum annuity term of 10 years, disallow any decline in the annuity, and require a non-zero remainder interest. The Administration estimates this proposal would raise $3 billion over 10 years.

Minority Discounts

There are existing restrictions to keep estates from engaging in artificial actions designed to reduce the value of estates (such as freezes on assets). As discussed above, courts sometimes allow estates to reduce the fair market value when assets are left in family partnerships where no one has a majority control. These discounts have even been allowed when assets are in cash and readily marketable securities, and the setting up of these family partnerships has become an estate tax avoidance tool. A provision in the Administration's proposal would set up a category of disregarded actions that could not be used to allow discounts. The estimated revenue gain is $18.7 billion over 10 years.

Consistent Valuation

There is no explicit rule preventing a low valuation of fair market value for an estate and a high valuation of the asset for purposes of stepped up basis in the hands of the heir. A provision in the Administration's budget proposals would require this value to be the same and is projected to raise $3 billion over 10 years.

CONCLUSION

The analysis indicates that the estate tax is relatively small, in revenues, in coverage, and in its effects on family businesses, savings, charitable contributions, and tax administration and compliance. One-fourth of 1% or less of all estates and of family businesses are expected to be subject to tax under an exemption of $3.5 million or $5 million. This share would grow slightly over the 10-year budget horizon, but indexing the exemption would not be very important over this short time period.

The estate tax is a small, but highly progressive, element of the tax system. Under the proposals under consideration (the $3.5 million exemption and the $5 million exemption), the majority of the tax falls on estates of $20 million or more, which in turn constitute only three-hundredths of 1% of decedents. For the $3.5 million exemption, 45% rate effective in 2009, 96% of the tax falls on the top quintile of the income distribution, 72% falls in the top 1%, and 42% in the top 0.1%.

Effects on savings are uncertain in direction but likely small. Based on empirical evidence, a decline of 1% to 2% in charitable contributions from increasing the estate tax relative to the current law baseline of a $1 million exemption with a 55% rate would be expected. Costs of estate planning and administration are relatively small as a percentage of estate tax revenue.

Because transfers between spouses are exempt, allowing spouses to inherit the exemption can increase the combined couples' exemption, and simplify estate planning. This change could cost increasing amounts of revenue over time, however, and lead to certain administrative complications.

Several provisions to deal with perceived abuses might be considered, with the most important one relating to the use of discounts when assets are left to a family partnership and no one heir controls the property.

End Notes

[1] See Chuck O'Toole, "Estate Tax Expiration Imminent After Congress Fails to Complete Action," *Tax Notes Today*, December 17, 2009, 2009TNT 240-4. For a discussion indicating that there would not be a legal issue with a retroactive tax, see Jay Starkman, "Can an Estate Tax be Retroactive?" *Tax Notes*, February 22, 2010, pp. 972-974.

[2] In addition to H.R. 4154, numerous bills were introduced in the 111th Congress to address the estate tax. See CRS Report R40964, *Estate Tax Legislation in the 111th Congress*, by Nonna A. Noto. The phase-in proposal was described in Martin Vaughn, U.S. Effort to Reduce Estate Tax Hits Turbulance, Dow Jones Newswire, May 18, 2010, posted at http://www.nasdaq.com/aspx/stock-market-news-story.aspx?storyid=201005181832dowjonesdjonline 000463&title=us-senate-effort-to-reduce-estate-tax-hits-turbulence.

[3] CRS Report 95-416, *Federal Estate, Gift, and Generation-Skipping Taxes: A Description of Current Law*, by John R. Luckey provides a detailed description of the estate tax.

[4] For example, parents may directly skip a generation by leaving some assets to grandchildren, or they may set up a lifetime trust for their children, with the assets subsequently inherited by the grandchildren. The generation skipping tax is imposed in these circumstances, although it also has an exemption.

[5] To convert the statutory tax inclusive rate into an equivalent rate for a tax exclusive application, the formula is t/(1+t), where t is the tax inclusive rate.

[6] Leaders of both parties have indicated an intention to continue an estate tax, although some bills propose its permanent elimination. If the estate tax is eliminated, the main options are whether or not to continue the gift tax and the carryover basis for appreciated assets. In the absence of an estate tax, a gift tax can limit certain abuses that can arise from the transfer of assets between taxpayers with differing tax rates. These issues are not discussed in detail in this report.

[7] William G. Gale and Joel Slemrod, "Rhetoric and Economics in the Estate Tax Debate," *National Tax Journal*, vol. 54, September 2001, pp. 613-627.

[8] These Treasury and JCT numbers are reported on a year-by-year basis in CRS Report R40964, *Estate Tax Legislation in the 111th Congress*, by Nonna A. Noto.

[9] The corporate tax is estimated to have a similar amount of concentration at higher income levels as the estate tax at the $1 million exemption level; the $3.5 million level is more concentrated. The individual income tax is more progressive at the lower end of the distribution, however, because it provides subsidies. For comparisons of taxes see Urban Brooking Tax Policy Center Table T09-0373 http://www.taxpolicycenter.org/numbers/displayatab.cfm?DocID=2448&topic2ID=40&topic3ID=81&DocTypeID=.

[10] Michael J. Graetz and Ian Shapiro, *Death by a Thousand Cuts: The Fight Over Taxing Inherited Wealth*, Princeton, N.J. Princeton University Press, 2005.

[11]See CRS Report RS20593, *Asset Distribution of Taxable Estates: An Analysis*, by Steven Maguire. Assets counted as business include closely held stock , real estate partnerships, other limited partnerships, farm assets, and other non-corporate business assets. If real estate and limited partnerships are excluded, the share is 14%.

[12] Ron Durst, *Federal Tax Policies and Farm Households*, U.S. Department of Agriculture, Economic Information Bulletin 54, Mau 2009, http://www.ers.usda. gov/ Publications/ EIB54/EIB54.pdf.

[13] The number of farms reported in the USDA study are 2.022 million, and if the average death to population ratio (about 0.008) were applied, the number of total farm decedents would be about 17,000. The 123 returns reported by CBO are about 0.7% of this number.

[14] See CRS Report RL33070, *Estate Taxes and Family Businesses: Economic Issues*, by Jane G. Gravelle and Steven Maguire for a discussion of business deduction options.

[15] Wojciech Kopczuk and Joel Slemrod, "The Impact of the Estate Tax on the Wealth Accumulation and Avoidance Behavior of Donors," Working Paper 7960, National Bureau of Economic Research, October 2000.

[16] Douglas Holtz-Eakin and Cameron T. Smith. "Changing Views of the Estate Tax: Implications for Legislative Options," American Family Business Foundation, February 2009.

[17] Unfortunately, the study did not spell out the methodology used in detail, including not identifying precisely what elasticity was used or how the price and income effects were measured.

[18] Based on CBO data the estate tax collected $26 billion in that year, while the corporate tax collected $370 billion and capital gains $126 billion (Congressional Budget Office, The Budget and Economic Outlook for FY2010-FY2019, January 2010, http://www.cbo.gov/ftpdocs/108xx/doc10871/01-26-Outlook.pdf). From individual tax return data an additional $121 billion is estimated from the individual income tax (a 15% tax on qualified dividends, a 20% tax on other income including interest, rent, and business income). The estimate assumes that 25% of business income is a return to capital. Data from Internal Revenue Service, Statistics of Income, Individual Income Tax Returns, located at http://www.irs.gov/taxstats/.

[19] Based on a typical rule of thumb that the capital stock is 3.5 times output, the capital stock would be around $40 billion. Note that a different functional form, such as a constant elasticity function, could alter the projection but not the general magnitude.

[20] See Eric Engen, Jane Gravelle, and Kent Smetters, "Dynamic Tax Models: Why They Do the Things They Do" *National Tax Journal* , vol. 50, September 1997, pp. 657-682. Results from eliminating capital income taxes ranged from a 1% fall in the capital stock to a 34% rise.

[21] In technical terms, the estimate appears to have been made solely from looking at the supply curve and did not take account of the demand curve. The elasticity of the demand curve for capital with respect to the rate of return is the factor substitution elasticity divided by the labor income share of output, and multiplied by the rate of return, divided by the rate of return plus depreciation. The factor substitution elasticity is generally one or less in absolute value (the elasticity is negative), the labor share about two-thirds, and the ratio of return to return plus depreciation about 0.7 making the absolute value of the demand elasticity of capital 1.05 or less. Since the total elasticity is the demand elasticity times the supply elasticity, all divided by the sum of the absolute value of the two elasticities, and the calculations imply that the supply elasticity is about 2.22, the inclusion of demand effects would have reduced the projection by over two-thirds.

[22] CRS Report R40518, *Charitable Contributions: The Itemized Deduction Cap and Other FY2011 Budget Options*, by Jane G. Gravelle and Donald J. Marples.

[23] William G. Gale and Joel Slemrod, "Rhetoric and Economics in the Estate Tax Debate," *National Tax Journal*, vol. 54, September 2001, pp. 613-627.

[24] These issues do not exhaust the possible reforms that might be considered. See CRS Report RL30600, *Estate and Gift Taxes: Economic Issues*, by Donald J. Marples and Jane G. Gravelle, pp. 22-24.

[25] Joint Committee on Taxation, *Taxation of Wealth Transfers Within A Family: A Discussion of Selected Areas for Possible Reform*, JCX-23-08, http://www.jct.gov/publications.html?func=startdown&id=1317.

[26] See also William J. Turnier, "Three Equitable Taxpayer-Friendly Reforms of Estate and Gift Taxation," *Tax Notes*, April 10, 2000, pp. 269-279.

[27] For a discussion of these and other proposals, see the "Green Book": *General Explanations of the Administrations Fiscal Year 2011 Revenue Proposals*, February 2010, http://www.reas.gov/offices/tax-policy/library/greenbk10.pdf.

In: Estate and Gift Taxes
Editor: Jacob A. Hughes

ISBN: 978-1-62100-516-2

Chapter 3

A HISTORY OF FEDERAL ESTATE, GIFT, AND GENERATION-SKIPPING TAXES*

John R. Luckey

SUMMARY

In 2010, the first year since 1916, there was no federal estate tax. There was also a year hiatus for the generation-skipping tax. The Economic Growth and Tax Relief Reconciliation Act of 2001 (P.L. 107-16) provided for a phaseout of the estate and generation-skipping taxes over a 10-year period, leaving the gift tax as the only federal transfer tax in 2010. The Tax Relief, Unemployment Insurance Reauthorization, and Job Creation Act of 2010 (P.L. 111-312) marked, at least, the suspension, if not the termination, of the movement away from the transfer taxes. The act temporarily (through the end of 2012) reinstated the estate and generation-skipping taxes with lower top rates (35%) and larger exemptions ($5,000,000) and reunified the estate and gift taxes. The act was effective on January 1, 2011, but estates of decendents dying in 2010 were given the option of electing coverage by the reinsted estate tax or keeping the carry-over basis for inherited assets.

In this report, the history of the federal transfer taxes has been divided into five parts: (1) the federal death and gift taxes used between 1789 and 1915; (2) the development, from 1916 through 1975, of the modern estate and gift taxes; (3) the creation and refinement of a unified

* This is an edited, reformatted and augmented version of a Congressional Research Service publication, CRS Report for Congress 95-444, from www.crs.gov, dated January 24, 2011.

estate and gift tax system, supplemented by a generation-skipping transfer tax; (4) the phaseout and repeal of the estate and generation-skipping taxes, with the gift tax being retained as a device to protect the integrity of the income tax; and (5) the return of the full complement of transfer taxes with lower top rates and larger exemptions.

INTRODUCTION

The concept of a death tax and the controversies surrounding such taxes have ancient roots. There is evidence of a 10% tax on transfers of property at death in ancient Egypt, as early as 700 B.C.[1] Later, the Greeks and Romans adopted death taxes. Critics of such taxes may trace their grievances at least to Pliny the Younger, who charged that a death tax was "an unnatural tax augmenting the grief and sorrow of the bereaved."[2]

The gift tax has developed as a necessary concomitant to the death tax because the easiest way to escape a tax on the gratuitous transfer of property at death is to divest oneself of the property during life. The impact of either tax alone would be diminished by the escape offered by the alternate transfer.[3]

Starting in 1976, Congress almost completely restructured the federal transfer tax system. The estate and gift taxes were unified. The scope of these taxes was changed in terms of size of estates affected. Perceived loopholes of major importance were closed or narrowed. Certain groups, previously thought to have suffered excessive tax burdens, were afforded relief. A new tax, the generation-skipping transfer tax, was added to supplement these two other transfer taxes.

The enactment of the Economic Growth and Tax Relief Reconciliation Act of 2001[4] culminated a movement away from the use of transfer taxes. The act phased out the estate and generation-skipping taxes over a 10- year period, leaving the gift tax as the only federal transfer tax. In 2010, the first year since 1916, there was no federal estate tax. There was also a year hiatus for the generation-skipping tax.

The Tax Relief, Unemployment Insurance Reauthorization, and Job Creation Act of 2010[5] marked, at least, the suspension, if not the termination, of this movement away from the transfer taxes. The act temporarily (through the end of 2012) reinstated the estate and generation-skipping taxes with lower top rates and larger exemptions and reunified the estate and gift taxes.

This report details the history of the three federal transfer taxes, tracing their development from their 18th-century roots to the present.[6]

DEATH AND GIFT TAXES IN THE UNITED STATES: 1789-1915

Prior to 1916, the United States did not make regular use of death and gift taxes. The federal government turned to them only in time of extraordinary revenue demands, such as wartime, although individual states used them extensively.

The Death Stamp Tax: 1789-1802

The federal experience with death taxes began in the eighteenth century, when strained trade relations with France necessitated development of a strong naval force. In 1794, a special revenue committee of the House of Representatives recommended that a system of stamp duties be adopted to meet the resultant revenue needs. The recommended duties included a tax:

> On inventories of the effects of deceased persons, ten cents.
>
> On receipts for legacies, or shares of personal estate, where the sum is above \$50 and not exceeding \$100, twenty-five cents; more than \$100 and not exceeding \$500, fifty cents; for every further sum above \$500, a dollar. Not to extend to wives, children or grandchildren.
>
> On probates of wills, and letters of administration, fifty cents.[7]

In 1796, the House Committee on Ways and means reported to Congress a bill to adopt such a tax[8] and the tax was enacted in 1797.

The Stamp Act of July 6, 1797,[9] required the use of federal stamps on receipts and discharges from legacies and intestate shares, and levied a charge for the purchase of the required stamps. The rate structure recommended by the special revenue committee in 1794 was adopted, along with exemptions for distributions to a wife (but not a husband), or a child or grandchild.[10] The stamp tax continued in force until 1802, when it was repealed.[11] For the next 60 years, the federal tax structure endured without any form of death tax.

The Civil War Inheritance Taxes: 1862-1870

The Civil War period was important in the development of the federal estate and gift tax system. The Revenue Act of 1862 introduced the first federal gift tax and included a number of features that have become important parts of the present federal estate, gift, and generation-skipping tax laws, including taxation of certain lifetime transfers of a testamentary character and exemption of small estates. During the debate on the act, Congress considered for the first time special treatment of charitable transfers.[12]

The use of a federal death tax was revived in 1862 to meet the revenue demands of the Civil War.[13] The 1862 levy, like its predecessor, taxed legacies and distributive shares of personal property but, unlike its predecessor, it was not a documentary stamp tax but an inheritance tax (a tax imposed upon individuals who receive property from a decedent upon the privilege of inheriting the property).[14]

The amount of the 1862 tax was, as is typical of inheritance taxes, graduated according to the closeness of the familial relationship between the decedent and the beneficiary. The rates ranged from 0.75%, for distributions to ancestors, lineal descendants, and siblings, to 5%, for distributions to distant relations and unrelated persons. The tax was imposed only on personal estates in excess of $1,000. Bequests to surviving spouses were entirely exempt from tax. Gifts intended to take effect at the donor's death or thereafter were included in the donor's estate for tax purposes.

War revenue needs prompted Congress to increase the rates of tax on inheritances in 1864 and to impose a succession tax on the receipt of real property by devise. The succession tax applied both to devises of real property and to transfers for inadequate consideration, though transfers in consideration of marriage were regarded as transfers for adequate consideration. Widows (though not widowers) were exempt from the succession tax, and charitable transfers of real estate were expressly taxed at the highest rate.[15]

In 1866, Congress responded to pleas of the Special Commissioner of the Revenue and tightened enforcement of the legacy and succession taxes. A penalty of up to $1,000 was imposed on executors and administrators who failed to furnish the required statements or filed false statements.[16]

The legacy and succession taxes were repealed in 1870, when the need for their additional revenues had ceased.[17] Four years later, the United States Supreme Court held, in *Scholey v. Rew*,[18] that the legacy and succession taxes had been constitutionally imposed.

In *Scholey*, the taxpayer contended that the Civil War death taxes were direct taxes which, under the United States Constitution, must be apportioned according to the census.[19] The Court disagreed, stating that

> Taxes on lands, houses, and other permanent real estate have always been deemed to be direct taxes, and capitation taxes, by the express words of the Constitution, are within the same category, but it never has been decided that any other legal exactions for the support of the federal government fall within the condition that unless laid in proportion to the numbers that the assessment is invalid. Whether direct taxes in the sense of the Constitution comprehends any other tax than a capitation tax and a tax on land is a question not absolutely decided, nor is it necessary to determine it in the present case, as it is expressly decided that the term does not include tax on income, which cannot be distinguished in principle from succession tax such as the one in the present controversy.[20]

An Income Tax on Gifts and Inheritance: 1894

The Income Tax Act of 1894 was not, in a technical sense, a death or gift tax, but it did treat gifts and inheritances as income and tax them as such.[21] The tax was short-lived, as the United States Supreme Court ruled it unconstitutional in 1895, in *Pollock* v. *Farmers' Loan and Trust Company*.[22] The Court found that, to the extent the 1894 income tax was imposed on the gains from real estate, it so burdened the real estate as to constitute a direct tax, which had to be apportioned among the states according to the census. The Court struck down the entire statute because it found that elimination of only the tax on real estate income would unduly burden the other classes of income taxpayers, contrary to congressional intent.

Modified Estate Tax: 1898-1902

The War Revenue Act of 1898[23] imposed another death tax in order to raise revenues to finance the Spanish-American War. The 1898 death tax was a form of estate tax, levied upon the value of all personal property included in a decedent's gross estate. Property passing to a surviving spouse was excluded from the tax, and a $10,000 specific exemption excluded small estates. The tax rates were graduated from 0.74% to 15%, taking into consideration both the size of the estate and the degree of kinship of the decedent and the beneficiaries.

The United States Supreme Court upheld the 1898 estate tax in *Knowlton v. Moore*.[24] The Court reaffirmed its earlier decision in *Scholey v. Rew, supra*, and said that the estate tax, like the inheritance tax, was an indirect tax subject to the rule of uniformity and not the rule of apportionment. The Court rejected the contention that death taxes were the exclusive prerogative of the states and held that, although wills and distribution of estates were matters for state law, taxation of these transfers could rest with the federal government as well as the states.

The 1898 estates tax was amended in 1901 to exempt bequests to charitable, religious, literary and educational organizations and to organizations for the encouragement of the arts or the prevention of cruelty to children.[25] In 1902, the estate tax was repealed.[26]

Reasons for Federal Death Taxes: 1789-1915

Federal death taxes in the United States between 1797 and 1915 appear to have served as supplementary revenue sources adopted only during war times. There is little support for the theory that these taxes were levied in an attempt to prevent the transfer of vast estates or to redistribute wealth.

Attitudes began to change with respect to the perpetuation of large estates, however, and in a speech in 1906 President Theodore Roosevelt called for:

> a progressive tax on all fortunes beyond a certain amount, either given in life or devised or bequested upon death to any individual—a tax so framed as to put it out of the power of the owner of one of these enormous fortunes to hand on more than a certain amount to any one individual.[27]

Development of the Modern Federal Estate and Gift Taxes: 1916-1975

A history of the modern federal estate and gift taxes must begin in 1916. Though since extensively reexamined and revised numerous times, legislation enacted that year is the direct ancestor of current law.

The Revenue Act of 1916

In 1916, Congress reacted to a mixture of changing attitudes and revenue shortages, the latter caused by a reduction in United States trade tariff receipts in the early years of World War I. It became apparent that greater reliance would have to be placed on internal taxes and that dependence on tariffs would have to be reduced. One internal tax was a federal estate tax.

The estate tax adopted in the Revenue Act of 1916[28] had many features of the current taxes. It was measured by the value of the property owned by a decedent at the date of death and the value of a decedent's estate was increased for tax purposes by certain lifetime transfers, including transfers for inadequate consideration, transfers not intended to take effect until death, and transfers in contemplation of death.[29] The full value of property owned concurrently by a decedent and another person would be included in the decedent's gross estate, unless it could be established that the surviving joint owner had contributed part of the property's acquisition cost.

The 1916 estate tax allowed the executor to reduce a decedent's estate for tax purposes by a $50,000 exemption and the amount of any funeral expenses, administration expenses, debts, losses, and claims against the estate. The tax rates ranged from 1% on net estates of up to $50,000, to 10% on net estates over $5,000,000.

The Supreme Court upheld the 1916 estate tax in *New York Trust Company v. Eisner*.[30] Writing for the Court, Justice Oliver Wendell Holmes stated:

> The statement of the constitutional objections urged imports on its face a distinction that, if correct, evidently hitherto has escaped this Court. *See*, *United States v. Field*, 255 U.S. 257. It is admitted, as since *Knowlton v. Moore*, 178 U.S. 41, it has to be, that the United States has power to tax legacies, but it is said that this tax is cast upon a transfer while it is being effectuated by the State itself and therefore, is an intrusion upon its processes, whereas a legacy tax is not imposed until the process is complete. An analogy is sought in the difference between the attempt of a State to tax commerce among the States and its right after the goods have become mingled with the general stock in the State. A consideration of the parallel is enough to detect the fallacy. A tax that was directed solely against goods imported into the State and that was determined by the fact of importation would be no better after the goods were at rest in the State than before. It would be as much an interference with commerce in one case as in the other.... Conversely, if a tax on the property distributed by the laws of a State, determined by the fact that

distribution has been accomplished, is valid, a tax determined by the fact that distribution is about to begin is no greater interference and is equally good.[31]

Rate Increases: 1917

The revenue demands of defense preparations prompted increases of one-half in the estate tax rates, as part of the Revenue Act of 1917.[32] Later in that same year, two new rate brackets were added at the upper end of the rate scale.[33] By the end of 1917, the estate tax rates progressed from 2% on net estates below $50,000, to 22% on net estates between $8,000,000 and $10,000,000, and 25% on net estates above $10,000,000. Estates of individuals whose death resulted from military service were not taxed.

Estate Tax Fluctuations and a Brief Gift Tax: 1918-1926

The conclusion of World War I prompted debates over the continued existence of the estate tax. The House of Representatives approved a rate in 1918[34] but the Senate sought instead to replace the estate tax with an inheritance tax. The Revenue Act of 1918[35] reflected a compromise between the views of the House and Senate, retaining the estate tax but cutting the rates on estates of less than $1,000,000.

The 1918 law also expanded the estate tax base by including the value of a surviving spouse's dower or curtesy right in the decedent's estate and the proceeds, over $40,000, of life insurance policies on the decedent's life, if they were receivable by the executor or the estate. The 1918 Act also included in the gross estate the value of any property subject to a general power of appointment held by the decedent, whether exercised in the decedent's will or exercised during the decedent's life in contemplation of death.[36] Charitable contributions were deductible in computing the taxable estate.

The estate tax remained unchanged until 1924, when Congress again increased the estate tax rates to a top rate of 40% on net estates over $10,000,000; made certain adjustments to the estate tax base; and added a gift tax.[37] The estate tax base was increased by adding the value of property which a decedent transferred during life but over which the decedent retained the power to "alter, amend, or revoke" the beneficial enjoyment. Provision was also made for allocating to the estate a portion of the value of concurrently owned property acquired by a decedent and a surviving joint owner by gift or inheritance, in which case there would be no relative contributions. Also, a credit against the federal estate tax was allowed for state death taxes, up to a total of 25% of the federal tax liability.

The Revenue Act of 1924 also added a gift tax with the same rate schedule as the estate tax. A lifetime exclusion of $50,000 and an annual exclusion of $500 per donee were both allowed. Neither charitable contributions nor gifts of property which the donor had received by gift or inheritance within the past five years were subject to gift tax.

Stiff opposition to the estate and gift taxes increased during the mid-1920s, and in 1926 the gift tax and many of the estate tax rate increases were repealed.[38] The 1926 Act created an estate tax rate range from 1% on net estates under $50,000, to 20% on net estates above $10,000,000. The estate tax exemption was increased from $50,000 to $100,000, and the maximum credit for state death taxes was increased from 25% to 80% of the federal estate tax liability.

Although the 1924 gift tax was repealed by the Revenue Act of 1926, it did stimulate a decision of the United States Supreme Court upholding its constitutionality. In *Bromley v. McCaughn*,[39] the Court held that the gift tax was an excise tax of the constitutional class of indirect taxes, requiring only intrinsic uniformity, rather than apportionment.

Estate Tax Rate Increases and a Permanent Gift Tax: 1932-1941

The depression of the 1930s reduced income tax revenues and increased the demand for revenues to finance various new government projects. Again, Congress turned to the estate and gift taxes.

The Revenue Act of 1932[40] increased the estate tax rates at virtually every level, added two new rate brackets, and reduced the estate tax exemption to its 1924 level of $50,000. The resultant estate tax had rates graduated from 1% on net estates up to $100,000, to 45% on net estates above $10,000,000.

The 1932 Act also reintroduced a federal gift tax, but with rates set at three-quarters of the estate tax rates, a level maintained until 1976. The lifetime gift tax exclusion was set at $50,000, and the annual exclusion at $5,000 per donee. No tax was imposed on charitable gifts.

The gift tax was, and continues to be, cumulative. That is, the rate of tax on each successive taxable gift over the donor's lifetime is computed on the basis of the total amount of all such gifts. If two donors each made identical gifts of $50,000 in a specific year, the donor with the greater amount of lifetime taxable gifts (after 1932) would pay the higher tax on the present transfer.

Between 1934 and 1942, social policies and wartime demands led to a series of estate and gift tax rate increases, though the gift tax rates continued to be maintained at three-quarters of the estate tax rates. The Revenue Act of 1934 raised the maximum estate tax rate to 60%, on a net estate over $10,000,000,[41] and the Revenue Act of 1935 further raised it to 70%, on net estates over $50,000,000.[42] The 1935 Act also reduced the estate and gift tax lifetime exemptions to $40,000 each.

The outbreak of World War II in Europe raised congressional concern over the state of American military preparedness and prompted an increase in the estate and gift taxes to provide additional revenue. The Revenue Act of 1940 added a 10% surtax to the income, estate, and gift taxes.[43] The Revenue Act of 1941 increased the estate and gift tax rates even further, producing an estate tax rate graduation from 3%, on net estates not over $5,000, to 77%, on net estates over $50,000,000.[44] The gift tax rates were maintained at three-quarters of the estate tax rates.

Further Rate Adjustments and the Marital Deduction: 1942-1948

The basic estate and gift tax exemptions were altered again by the Revenue Act of 1942,[45] which created a $60,000 estate tax exemption, a $30,000 lifetime gift tax exclusion, and a $3,000 annual per donee gift tax exclusion. The 1942 Act also increased the estate tax base by including in a decedent's gross estate the proceeds of any life insurance policy on the decedent's life if either the proceeds were payable to or for the benefit of the estate or the decedent had paid the premiums on the policy.

The 1942 Act also attempted to correct the perceived inequity in estate and gift taxation between residents of community property states and non-community property states.[46] Property owned concurrently by a decedent and a surviving spouse in a non-community property state was excluded from the decedent's gross estate only to the extent it could be shown that the surviving spouse contributed to the acquisition cost. In a community property state, however, one-half of all property acquired by either spouse during their marriage belonged to each spouse, by operation of law. On the death of either spouse, only one-half of the community property would be subject to estate taxes.[47] This resulted in the automatic equalization of the estates of spouses residing in community property states and a lower total estate tax burden.

Congress attempted to resolve this problem by treating community property like it treated concurrently owned property in a non-community property state. Community property was included in a decedent's gross estate except to the extent that the surviving spouse could be shown to have contributed to the acquisition cost.

This solution, deemed complex and unsuccessful, was replaced in the Revenue Act of 1948[48] by the estate and gift tax marital deductions and the rules on split-gifts. The estate tax marital deduction permitted a decedent's estate to deduct the value of all property passing to a surviving spouse, whether passing under the will or otherwise. Under the 1948 Act, the maximum deduction was one-half of the decedent's adjusted gross estate (the gross estate less debts, taxes and administration expenses). Community property, however, was ineligible for the estate tax marital deduction, thereby equalizing the tax treatment of estates of residents of community property states and non-community property states.

The gift tax marital deduction allowed a donor to deduct one-half of an interspousal gift, other than community property, to a third person. Concomitantly, the split gift rule allowed the non-donor spouse to elect to be treated as having made a gift of one-half the total transfer. This election was to be made on the gift tax return, and use of two annual exclusions on gifts by a spouse to a third person was permitted.

Changes in the Estate Taxation of Life Insurance: 1954

The estate taxation of life insurance proceeds was changed during the recodification of the tax laws in 1954. The Internal Revenue Code of 1954 includes the proceeds of a life insurance policy on the decedent's life in the gross estate if the proceeds were payable to, or for the benefit of, the estate, if the decedent retained any incidents of ownership in the policy on the date of death, or if the decedent gave away any of the incidents of ownership in the policy within three years of death and in contemplation of death.[49]

Restructuring of the Federal Transfer Tax System: 1976-1998

Starting in 1976, Congress enacted major revisions to the federal transfer tax system. The estate and gift tax laws were significantly altered. A new tax on generation-skipping transfers was added.[50] The greatest structural change was the unification of the estate and gift taxes.

The Tax Reform Act of 1976

The Tax Reform Act of 1976[51] created a unified estate and gift tax framework, consisting of a single graduated rate of tax imposed on both lifetime gifts and testamentary dispositions. The gift tax remained cumulative, so that the rate of tax on each successive taxable gift was higher throughout the donor's entire lifetime. Transfers made at death are treated as the last taxable gift of the deceased donor. Therefore, the amount of lifetime taxable gifts affects the rate of tax imposed on the donor's taxable estate, though it does not affect the actual size of the taxable estate. The estate and gift tax rates were graduated to a maximum tax rate of 70% on cumulative gifts or taxable estates of more than $5,000,000.[52]

The Tax Reform Act of 1976 also merged the estate tax exclusion and the lifetime gift tax exclusion into a single, unified estate and gift tax credit,[53] which may be used to offset gift tax liability during the donor's lifetime but which, if unused at death, is available to offset the deceased donor's estate tax liability. The credit was $42,500 for transfers made in 1980 and $47,000 for transfers made after 1980. This was equivalent to an estate and gift tax exemption of $161,000 for transfers made during 1980 and $175,625 for transfers made after 1980.[54] The $3,000 per donee annual gift tax exclusion was retained unchanged.

The Tax Reform Act of 1976 also changed the income tax consequences of a sale of property received from a decedent. The gain on a sale is the difference between the amount realized by the seller and the seller's basis. An heir's basis in inherited property, prior to the 1976 Act, was its fair market value for federal estate tax purposes. Therefore, if inherited property were sold soon after the date of death, there would be no gain and no income tax liability. The appreciation accruing prior to the date of death would be forever eliminated from the income tax base. The 1976 Act provided a rule under which the basis of property received from a decedent was "carried over" from the decedent. This so-called "carryover basis" rule gave heirs a basis in inherited property equal to the decedent's basis on the date of death, with adjustments for a share of the appreciation accruing before 1977, a share of the estate taxes paid on the property, and a share of the state death taxes imposed on the property. The heir could also increase the basis in all of the decedent's property to a minimum basis of $60,000.[55]

The 1976 Act also increased the limitation on the estate tax marital deductions for moderate-sized estates, allowing the deduction for the greater of one-half of the adjusted gross estate (the former limitation) or $250,000.[56] In conjunction with the unified transfer tax credit, the increased estate tax marital deduction permitted the tax-free passage of an estate of up to $425,625 in 1981, if at least $250,000 passed to the surviving spouse.

The limitation on the gift tax marital deduction was also increased in certain cases, allowing a donor spouse to deduct the full amount of the first $100,000 of lifetime interspousal taxable gifts after 1976, but allowing no deduction on the next $100,000 of interspousal taxable gifts. A deduction was allowed for one-half of the value of all subsequent interspousal taxable gifts.[57]

The inclusion of property transferred by gift in contemplation of death was also revised by the 1976 Act, eliminating the rebuttable presumption that all gifts made within three years of death were made in contemplation of death. Now, the 1976 Act required automatic inclusion in the gross estate of the value of all gifts made within three years of death, unless they were less than $3,000.[58]

The 1976 Act also provided a method by which spouses could assure the exclusion of one-half of the value of concurrently owned property by electing to treat the creation of the joint interest as a taxable gift.[59] Previously, a gift to a spouse of one-half of the value of concurrently owned property did not remove any portion of the value of the property from the donor's gross estate, if the donor predeceased. Under the "fractional interest" rule, however, if the creation of the concurrently owned property was a taxable gift, and if certain other requirements were met, the estate of the first spouse to die included only one-half of the value of the concurrently owned property. Therefore, the executor did not have to establish relative contributions of the deceased and the surviving spouse.

The 1976 Act provided special rules for estates composed principally of interests in a closely held business or family farm. If the business (or farm) interest was a sufficiently large share of the estate, and if it satisfied certain other requirements, any real estate used in the farm or business will be valued at its present use, rather than its "highest and best use."[60] This provision could reduce the size of the decedent's gross estate by up to $500,000, but any estate tax savings were recaptured if the business or farm was not continued by the decedent's family for the next 15 years.

The 1976 Act also permitted estates composed primarily of an interest in a closely-held business or family farm to defer payment of the estate taxes attributable to the business interest.[61] If certain rules were met regarding the size of the business interest in proportion to the estate, no portion of the estate taxes attributable to the business interest would have to be paid for the first five years, with only interest required. The estate taxes on this share of the estate were allowed to be paid in up to ten equal annual installments thereafter.

The 1976 Act also created an estate tax deduction for certain bequests to minor children of the decedent if the children had no other living parents after the decedent's death. This "orphan's deduction" was limited to $5,000 for each year each child is under 21 years of age.[62]

One of the major changes in the 1976 Act was the adoption of a new tax on certain generation-skipping transfers. A generation-skipping transfer was defined as one which split the enjoyment and ownership of property between two individuals. The first level of beneficiaries, usually the donor's children, received the right to use and benefit from property during their lifetime. The second level of beneficiaries, usually the settlor's grandchildren, received the out-right ownership of the property at the termination of the interests of the first level of beneficiaries. Prior to the 1976 Act, the character of the interests held by the different beneficiaries had resulted in estate or gift taxation of the property to the donor and the ultimate, second level of beneficiaries, but not the intervening, first level of beneficiaries. The Tax Reform Act of 1976 added a complex series of rules designed to treat the termination of the interest of the intervening beneficiaries as a taxable event, taxed at a rate equal to the estate and gift tax rates which would have been applicable had the property been transferred outright by the donor and then by the first beneficiary.[63]

The Revenue Act of 1978

The Revenue Act of 1978[64] made a number of technical changes in the estate and gift tax rules added in 1976, and two substantive changes. First, it suspended the effective date of the carryover basis rules until 1980. Second, it provided a set of rules by which a surviving spouse who "materially participated" in the operation of a family firm or closely held business owned concurrently with a deceased spouse, could treat a portion of appreciation in the value of the business that accrued during the period of such participation, as cash consideration contributed by that surviving spouse. Therefore, a share of the value of the concurrently owned business assets would not be taxable in the estate of the deceased spouse because it would be treated as having come from the surviving spouse's contributions.[65]

The Crude Oil Windfall Profits Tax Act of 1980

The Crude Oil Windfall Profits Tax Act of 1980[66] is, perhaps, an odd vehicle for an important death tax provision. However, it was as an amendment to this bill that the carryover basis rules of the Tax Reform Act of 1976 were repealed, retroactive to the effective date of the 1976 Act.[67]

The Economic Recovery Tax Act of 1981

The Economic Recovery Act of 1981 (ERTA)[68] made substantial changes in the estate tax apparently designed to reduce the number of taxable estates and to prevent the imposition of an estate or gift tax on interspousal transfers. With only minor exceptions, these changes applied to estates of decedents dying after December 31, 1981, and to gifts made after December 31, 1981.

ERTA increased the unified transfer tax credit from $47,000 to $192,800, phased-in over six years, effectively increasing the exemption equivalent from $175,625 to $600,000 over that period.[69] Also phased-in over a three-year period was a reduction, from 70% to 50%, in the top estate, gift, and generation-skipping transfer tax rates applicable to transfers above $2,500,000.[70]

ERTA made substantial changes in the marital deduction. The quantitative limits on the estate and gift tax marital deductions were eliminated, thereby allowing unlimited interspousal tax-free transfers after December 31, 1981. The marital deduction was permitted for transfers of certain lifetime income interests in trust or otherwise, if the donor or executor elects to include the full value of the transferred property in the estate of the donee or surviving spouse. Transfers of income interests in charitable remainder trusts after December 31, 1981, were allowed to qualify for the marital deduction.[71]

A new rule was enacted regarding the estate taxation of property owned jointly by spouses with a right of survivorship. This rule required including in the gross estate of a decedent dying after December 31, 1981, only one-half of the value of property owned jointly with a right of survivorship by the decedent and the surviving spouse and no other persons, regardless of the relative contributions of the decedent and the surviving spouse. The 1981 Act also repeals the special rules that formerly applied with respect to elective fractional interests of a husband and wife in a jointly owned property and to jointly owned farm or business property.[72]

ERTA liberalized and simplified the rules by which an estate qualifies to have family farm or closely held business real estate valued at its present use, rather than its highest and best use. Included was a special rule to enable individuals more easily to retire on Social Security without losing the ability to specially value their farm or business real estate. The "material participation" standard was reduced in certain cases, and the amount by which a decedent's gross estate can be reduced by special use valuation was increased from $500,000 to $750,000. These rules apply generally with respect to estates of decedents dying after December 31, 1981.[73]

ERTA also liberalized and simplified the rules by which the estate taxes attributable to an interest in a closely held business can be paid in installments over a 15-year period. A special 4% interest rate on the deferred tax attributable to the first $1,000,000 in value was provided, with respect to estates of decedents dying after December 31, 1981.[74] The new law also eliminates the former 10- year installment payment rule.

After 1981, the rule by which property given away within three years of the date of death is automatically included in the gross estate of the donor was eliminated for most types of gifts. The automatic inclusion rule was retained in certain special instances, such as gifts of life insurance policies.[75]

ERTA increased the annual gift tax per donee exclusion from $3,000 to $10,000, with respect to taxable gifts after December 31, 1981. The act also permitted an unlimited annual exclusion for the payment of a donee's tuition or medical expenses.[76]

Only an annual gift tax return was required to be filed after 1981. The filing date for this return was set on the same date as the donor's income tax return, including time for extensions.[77]

A qualified disclaimer for estate and gift tax purposes was permitted even if the disclaimer was invalid under applicable state law, if the disclaimant actually transferred the property to the person who would have taken it if the disclaimer had been valid.[78]

ERTA repealed the orphan's deduction allowed first under the Tax Reform Act of 1976.[79] It also delayed for an additional year the effective date of the generation-skipping transfer tax rules with regard to transfers under wills and revocable trusts in existence on June 11, 1976.[80]

The Deficit Reduction Act of 1984

The Deficit Reduction Act of 1984 (DFRA)[81] contained a number of changes involving gift and estate taxes, though the essential thrust of the Economic Recovery Tax Act was unaffected.[82] DFRA froze the maximum gift and estate tax rate at 1984 levels (55%) until 1988. Under ERTA the top rate was scheduled to fall to the 50% level in 1985.[83]

DFRA modified the gift and estate tax law to liberalize provisions for gift tax free transfers to former spouses pursuant to a written agreement. It increased to three years, two years before and one year after a divorce, the period for making an agreement for such transfers. It also allowed an estate tax deduction for such transfers.[84]

DFRA made three changes that affected estates containing closely held businesses. First, it modified the installment payment provisions applicable to a closely held business interest to permit their use in a modified form where non-readily tradeable stock is indirectly owned. This was accomplished by permitting a look through a passive holding company to determine if the decedent owned 20% or more of the voting stock and the value of such closely held business interest exceeded 35% of the adjusted value of the estate.[85] Second, the alternate valuation rules were amended to permit an election on late returns, those filed within one year of the due date, and to prevent use of alternate valuation except where it resulted in a decrease in both the total value of the estate and estate taxes.[86] Third, a provision to permit perfection of a current use valuation election notice or agreement, where there was substantial compliance with IRS regulations in the original notice or agreement, was enacted.[87]

In DFRA, Congress, for the first time, adopted statutory provisions governing gift loans (certain below market interest rate loans) that treat foregone interest as a gift. An exception was provided where loans do not exceed $100,000. The act also provided for income tax treatment of the imputed interest.[88]

DFRA also provided for the addition of permanent rules for permitting reformation of a charitable, split-interest trust, to comply with the 1969 Tax Reform Act requirements for income, estate, or gift tax deductibility as a charitable contribution (Congress had in the past enacted temporary provisions permitting reformation);[89] elimination of the $100,000 estate tax exclusion for certain retirement benefits payable at death from individual retirement accounts, qualified plans, military retirement, and tax sheltered annuities;[90] and clarification of congressional intent to apply transfer taxes (gift, estate, and generation-skipping) to certain bonds exempt from income tax by virtue of law outside the Internal Revenue Code.[91]

The Tax Reform Act of 1986

The Tax Reform Act of 1986[92] contained four generally applicable changes to the estate, gift, and generation-skipping taxes. The most extensive of these changes was the repeal of the existing generation-skipping transfer tax retroactive to June 11, 1976, and enactment of a new system to tax such transfers.[93] This new tax replaced the graduated tax, based on the estate tax rates, with a flat rate tax set at the highest estate tax rate, currently 55%. The tax was applicable to all generation-skipping transfers, including transfers which directly skipped a generation without the intervening generation enjoying any beneficial interest in the transferred property.[94]

The Tax Reform Act also included a 50% exclusion from estate taxation of qualified proceeds from qualified sales of employer securities to an employee stock option plan;[95] modification of the definition of the qualified conservation contribution rules to allow a deduction without regard to whether contributions met the "conservation purpose" requirement of the income tax;[96] and repeal of the gift tax exclusion for an employee's exercise or non-exercise of an election under which an annuity, pension from a qualified plan, tax-deferred annuity, IRA, or military pension would be paid to a beneficiary after the employee's death.[97]

The Omnibus Budget Reconciliation Act of 1987

The Omnibus Budget Reconciliation Act of 1987 (OBRA)[98] contained four amendments to the estate, gift and generation-skipping taxes. The first of these amendments froze the generation-skipping tax rate and the top gift and estate tax rates at 55%, delaying the drop to a 50% rate until after December 31, 1992.[99]

OBRA provided for a phase-out of the unified credit for estate and gift transfers exceeding $10,000,000. This phase-out is accomplished by adding a

5% tax to the tax on taxable transfers over this amount until the benefit of the unified credit has been recaptured. Thus between 1988 and the end of 1992, transfers between $10,000,000 and $21,040,000 would be taxed at 60%. Once the recapture is complete, 55% would again become the tax rate. After 1992, when the top rate was scheduled to drop to 50%, the recapture was to apply to transfers between $10,000,000 and $18,340,000.[100] This provision did not affect the tax rate for computing the generation-skipping transfer tax.[101]

OBRA closed a perceived loophole which had been created by the provision of the Tax Reform Act of 1986, which established the estate tax deduction for sales of employer securities to an ESOP. This provision had left open the possibility that an estate could, through a series of purchases and sales to an ESOP, totally wipe out its estate tax liability. The act clarifies and restricts the availability of this deduction by limiting the deduction to sales of nonpublicly traded securities; limiting the deduction to 50% of the taxable estate; limiting the maximum reduction in estate taxes to $750,000; imposing holding requirements on the decedent and the ESOP; prohibiting the deduction in the case of securities acquired with assets transferred from another plan of the employer; and imposing an excise tax on the ESOP for failure to satisfy the allocation and holding period requirements.[102]

Finally, OBRA provided that "valuation" or "estate freeze" transactions will cause the total value of the property transferred in the transaction to be included in the decedent's gross estate as property in which the decedent had a retained interest.[103]

The Technical and Miscellaneous Revenue Act of 1988

The Technical and Miscellaneous Revenue Act of 1988 (TAMRA)[104] contained a number of amendments to the estate, gift, and generation-skipping taxes. Many of these, as the name of the act implies, were technical in nature. Among these were a number of clarifying amendments to the generation-skipping transfer tax, which affected such areas as the overlapping definitions of "direct skips," "taxable terminations," and "taxable distributions"; the inclusion ratio for charitable lead trusts and nontaxable gifts; generation assignment; taxation rules for multiple skips; and the grandchild exemption.[105]

TAMRA made several changes expanding and clarifying the situations to which the estate freeze rules apply.[106] The act also removed the marital deduction for both the estate and the gift tax when a spouse is not a citizen of the United States unless the transfer is made utilizing a "qualified domestic trust."[107]

TAMRA amended the alternate valuation rules for family farms. Under the amendment, a surviving spouse may rent the farm to a family member on a net cash basis without incurring recapture liability. The amendment applied to rentals occurring after December 31, 1976. The statute of limitations for refunds for closed years was waived for claims made within one year of TAMRA's enactment.[108]

Under prior law, art loaned to a tax-exempt organization was a transfer taxable under the gift tax. Such a transfer did not qualify for the gift tax charitable deduction because only a partial interest was transferred. TAMRA allowed such loans to qualify for the charitable deduction if the charities use of the art is related to the organizations tax-exempt purpose.[109]

The Revenue Reconciliation Act of 1989

The Revenue Reconciliation Act of 1989 (RRA)[110] contained a small number of amendments to the transfer taxes. The amendments to the generation-skipping tax were of a technical nature.[111] The gift tax was amended to allow the $100,000 exclusion for transfers to a noncitizen spouse only if the transfer would qualify for the marital deduction if the spouse were a citizen of the United States.[112]

The estate tax changes in RRA modified the new rules enacted in TAMRA concerning transfers to a spouse who is not a citizen of the United States. Under TAMRA the estate tax marital deduction had been eliminated for transfers to a noncitizen spouse unless a qualified domestic trust was utilized. The RRA allowed the use of the marital deduction for transfers to a resident spouse if the spouse became a citizen before the filing estate tax return.[113]

The RRA also modified the requirements of a qualified domestic trust. As modified, a qualified domestic trust needed only to have one trustee who is a citizen of the United States as opposed to the previous requirement that all trustees be citizens. The lone citizen trustee was required to have veto power over the distributions from the trust. Under the RRA, the noncitizen spouse no longer needed an income interest in the trust for the trust to be qualified, unless the trust was a terminable interest.[114]

The RRA went a long way toward taxing qualified domestic trusts in the same manner as the estates of citizen spouses by permitting certain estate tax benefits against the estate tax required of a qualified domestic trust upon the death of the noncitizen spouse. These benefits included alternate valuation, charitable deductions, special use valuation, and certain capital gains provisions.[115]

The RRA provided that the denial of the marital deduction to a noncitizen spouse will not be effective, during a three-year period from the effective date of the RRA, against a noncitizen spouse who is domiciled in a country which has a treaty with the United States which would provide a different result.[116] The RRA set rules and time tables for reforming trusts to qualify as qualified domestic trusts.[117]

The Omnibus Reconciliation Act of 1990

The Omnibus Budget Reconciliation Act of 1990 (OBRA90)[118] contained one modification of the estate and gift tax provisions. OBRA90 completely altered the transfer tax approach to the estate tax freeze which had been enacted in 1987 and amended in 1988. The previous approach to tax avoidance through freeze transactions was to include the at death value of property transferred in this manner in the estate of the transferor as a retained interest.[119] OBRA90 repealed section 2036(c) retroactively to 1987, thus removing the freeze transaction from the estate tax retained interest rules.[120]

Under OBRA90 the focus changed from the estate tax to the gift tax. The act added new rules for determining if the transfer constituted a gift and, if so, valuating the transferred interest at the time of the freeze transaction for gift tax purposes. These new rules were premised upon the general principal that the value of a residual interest is determined by subtracting the value of any retained interests from the value of the entire business entity, adjusted to reflect percentage of ownership or control. OBRA90 changed the gift tax consequences of the freeze transaction by establishing the value of the rights retained in the transaction at zero or a much lower value than that which would have been found under prior law, thus greatly increasing the value of the transferred (gifted) interest.[121]

The Omnibus Reconciliation Act of 1993

The Omnibus Budget Reconciliation Act of 1993[122] amended the transfer taxes by restoring[123] the top two tax rates to 53% and 55%, effective retroactively to December 31, 1992.[124]

The Taxpayer Relief Act of 1997

The Taxpayer Relief Act of 1997 (TRA)[125] amended all three of the transfer taxes. The unified credit was increased for the first time since 1981. The terminology was changed from unified credit to applicable exclusion amount. TRA phased in an increase in this applicable exclusion amount from $600,000 in 1997 to $1,000,000 in 2006 (*See*, column 2 in chart below).[126] Although this amount was not indexed for inflation, TRA did bring indexation to the estate and gift taxes for the first time. The following amounts were indexed for inflation beginning in 1998: the $10,000 annual exclusion for gifts; the $750,000 ceiling on special use valuation; the $1,000,000 generation-skipping tax exemption; and the $1,000,000 ceiling on the value of a closely-held business eligible for special low interest rates.[127]

TRA created a new exclusion from the estate tax for qualified family-owned businesses. Under this exclusion the executor of a qualified estate was empowered to elect special estate tax treatment for qualified "family-owned business interests." This exclusion was limited to a total of $1,300,000 when combined with the applicable exclusion amount of the unified credit.[128] Thus the family-owned business exclusion was scheduled to decrease as the applicable exclusion amount increased.

The TRA defined "qualified estate" to be the estate of a U.S. citizen or resident of which the aggregate value of the decedent's qualified family-owned business interests that are passed to qualified heirs exceeds 50% of the decedent's adjusted gross estate.[129] "Qualified heir" was defined to include any individual who has been employed in the business for at least 10 years prior to the date of the decedent's death, and members of the decedent's family.[130] A "qualified family-owned business interest" was defined as any interest in a business with principal place of business in the U.S. if ownership of the business is held at least 50% by one family, 70% by two families, or 90% by three families, as long as the decedent's family owns at least 30% of the business.[131]

Table 1. Applicable Exclusion amount and Family-Owned Business Exclusion

Year	Applicable Exclusion amount	Business Exclusion	Total Exclusion
1998	$625,000	$675,000	$1,300,000
1999	$650,000	$650,000	$1,300,000
2000-1	$675,000	$625,000	$1,300,000
2002-3	$700,000	$600,000	$1,300,000
2004	$850,000	$450,000	$1,300,000
2005	$950,000	$350,000	$1,300,000
2006+	$1,000,000	$300,000	$1,300,000

To qualify for the beneficial treatment afforded family-owned businesses under TRA, the decedent (or a member of his family) was required to have owned and materially participated in the business for at least five of the eight years preceding the death of the decedent. Also, each qualified heir was required to materially participate in the business for at least five years of any eight year period within ten years following the decedent's death.[132]

Other changes in the transfer taxes found in TRA included a reduction in the interest rate on installment payments of estate taxes attributable to closely held businesses;[133] denial of revaluation of gifts for estate tax purposes after the expiration of the statute of limitations;[134] repeal of the throwback rules applicable to domestic trusts;[135] reduction in the estate tax for certain land subject to permanent conservation easements;[136] and modification of the generation-skipping transfer tax for transfers to individuals with deceased parents.[137]

The Internal Revenue Service Restructuring and Reform Act of 1998

In addition to clarifying and making several technical amendments to changes enacted in 1997, the Internal Revenue Service Restructuring and Reform Act of 1998[138] contained one more substantive amendment to the estate tax. This amendment converted the family-owned business exclusion into a deduction.[139] The act also coordinated this new deduction with the unified credit to increase benefits to the estates with qualified family-owned business interests as the unified credit increases. The act provided that if an executor elected to use the family-owned business deduction, the estate tax liability would be calculated as if the estate were allowed a maximum qualified business deduction of $675,000 and an applicable exclusion amount of $625,000, regardless of the year in which the decedent died. If the estate included less than the $675,000 of qualified family-owned business interests, the applicable exclusion amount is increased on a dollar for dollar basis, limited to the applicable exclusion amount generally available for the year of death.[140]

Phaseout and Repeal of the Federal Estate and Generation-Skipping Taxes under the Economic Growth and Tax Relief Reconciliation Act of 2001

The Economic Growth and Tax Relief Reconciliation Act of 2001[141] generally repealed the federal estate and generation-skipping transfer taxes at the end of the year 2009, after a phaseout of these taxes over the period 2002 to 2009. The gift tax was lowered and modified. New income tax carry-over basis rules for property received from a decedent were provided.

Repeal of the Estate and Generation-Skipping Transfer Taxes

The federal estate tax and the generation-skipping transfer tax were repealed for decedents dying or generation-skipping transfers made after December 31, 2009.[142]

Phaseout of the Estate and Generation-Skipping Transfer Taxes

The phaseout of the estate tax was accomplished primarily by adjusting three features of the tax. The top rate was gradually lowered.[143] The applicable exclusion amount was gradually raised.[144] The credit for death taxes (estate or inheritance taxes) paid to a state was gradually lowered and replaced by a deduction for such taxes.[145] Also, the 5% surtax used to recapture the benefits of the graduated tax rates on taxable estates of over $10,000,000 was repealed,[146] and, after the applicable exclusion amount had surpassed the $1,300,000 level used to protect family owned businesses, the family owned business deduction was repealed.[147]

Table 2. Schedule of Changes

Year	Top Rate	Applicable Exclusion Amount	Credit for State Death Tax	Other Scheduled Changes
2002	50%	$1,000,000	75% of current allowable credit.	Repeal of 5% surtax.
2003	49%	$1,000,000	50% of current allowable credit.	—
2004	48%	$1,500,000	25% of current allowable credit.	Repeal of family owned business deduction.
2005	47%	$1,500,000	Credit repealed. Deduction for tax paid to state.	—
2006	46%	$2,000,000	Deduction for tax paid to state.	—
2007	45%	$2,000,000	Deduction for tax paid to state.	—
2008	45%	$2,000,000	Deduction for tax paid to state.	—
2009	45%	$3,500,000	Deduction for tax paid to state.	—

The phaseout of the generation-skipping tax was accomplished primarily through lowering the rates and increasing the lifetime exemption. The generation-skipping transfer tax was imposed at the top rate of the estate tax.[148] Therefore, when the top rate of the estate tax was lowered under the act, it had the affect of lowering the generation-skipping tax as well. The lifetime exemption was increased by making the exemption equal to the estate tax applicable exclusion amount.[149]

Modification of the Gift Tax

The gift tax was retained in order to protect the integrity of the income tax. It was feared that, absent a gift tax, income producing property could be gifted to taxpayers in lower brackets, sold, the taxes paid, and the proceeds gifted back to the higher bracket taxpayer, thus avoiding great amounts of income tax on the sale of capital assets.

The gift tax was modified by lowering the rates and increasing the applicable exclusion amount. The top rate of the gift tax declined with the top rate of the estate tax.[150] After the repeal of the estate tax, the top gift tax rate was lowered to 35% of the excess over $500,000.[151] The applicable exclusion amount was raised to $1,000,000 in the year 2002. This amount remained constant through the phaseout period of the estate tax and through 2010.[152] Thus, when the applicable exclusion amount increased for the estate tax in the phaseout period, only $1,000,000 might be used to cover lifetime transfers (i.e., gifts).

Basis Rules for Property Received from a Decedent

Technically the carry-over basis rules were income tax rules, not estate tax rules. Basis is used to determine gain on the sale of capital assets for income tax purposes. Often basis and cost are equivalent. Generally, to determine taxable income from sale of a capital asset, the basis in that asset is subtracted from the sale price. Prior to and during the phaseout period, the basis in property received from a decedent was a "stepped-up" basis.[153] The inheritor of property, instead of having the basis of the one from which he received the property (a carry-over basis), had a basis in the property of the fair market value of the property at the date of death of the decedent. The purpose of the stepped-up basis rule was to avoid double taxation. The property had been subject to the estate tax. If the property had a carry-over basis and was sold after inheritance, there would be a capital gain subject to the income tax. The use of the stepped-up basis eliminated this capital gain and thus the income tax on the sale. With the repeal of the estate tax, this need for the stepped-up basis rules was removed.

The act repealed the stepped-up basis rule at the end of the year 2009 (when the estate tax was repealed).[154] The carry-over basis rule in effect for 2010 was the basis in property received from a decedent is the lesser of carry-over basis or the fair market value of the property on the date of death of the decedent.[155]

Under the estate tax and the income tax stepped-up basis rules, an amount of the gross estate was not subject to either tax.[156] To compensate for the loss of the exempt property with the repeal of the estate tax and the change to carry-over basis, the act provided for two amounts of property which were still to receive stepped-up basis. Every estate could allocate $1,300,000 basis increase to property in the taxable estate.[157] In addition to this general step-up, property which passed to the spouse of the decedent could be allocated up to $3,000,000 basis increase.[158] Each of these amounts was to be indexed for inflation.

Other Amendments

The act required certain new returns to be filed to provide information for administration of the new basis rules.[159]

The act removed the mileage restrictions for the estate tax rule for creation of conservation easements. This amendment applied to the estates of decedents dying after December 31, 2000.[160]

The act modified the generation-skipping transfer tax allocation rules for certain lifetime transfers to a trust.[161]

The Restoration: The Tax Relief, Unemployment Insurance Reauthorization, and Job Creation Act of 2010

The Tax Relief, Unemployment Insurance Reauthorization, and Job Creation Act of 2010 (the 2010 Act)[162] marked, at least, the suspension, if not the termination, of the movement away from the transfer taxes. The act temporarily (through the end of 2012) reinstated the estate and generation-skipping taxes with lower top rates and larger exemptions and reunified the estate and gift taxes.

Reinstatement of the Estate and Generation-Skipping Taxes; and Repeal of the Carry-over Basis

Section 301 of the 2010 Act reinstated the estate and generation-skipping taxes and repealed the carry-over basis rule which came into effect in 2010.[163] The full unified credit against the estate and gift taxes was restored.[164] A special irrevocable election was provided for estates of decedents who died in

2010. These estates could elect to have the estate tax, as reinstated (lower rates, higher exemption, and stepped-up basis), applied to the estate or it could elect to utilize the carryover basis rules which were in effect in 2010.[165] The generation-skipping tax was reinstated retroactively, [166] but the applicable rate for 2010 transfers was set at zero.[167]

Modifications to Estate and Gift Taxes

The 2010 Act altered the applicable exclusion amount in three ways. First, the applicable exclusion amount was raised to $5,000,000 (to be adjusted for inflation).[168] Second, the full applicable exclusion amount was, again, made available for use against the gift tax.[169] Third, a surviving spouse was permitted to utilize any unused exclusion amount of their spouse.[170]The top rate for all three transfer taxes was set at 35%.[171]

Sunset Rule

The sunset rule of the Economic Growth and Tax Relief Reconciliation Act of 2001[172] as amended by the 2010 Act[173] was made applicable to these transfer tax amendments.[174] In other words, the changes made to the transfer taxes will sunset at the end of 2012. Therefore, absent Congressional action in the interim, the law governing the estate, gift and generation-skipping transfer taxes will revert on January 1, 2013, to the law that was in place on June 7, 2001.

End Notes

[1] Randolph E. Paul, *Federal Estate and Gift Taxation*, p. 3 (Boston 1942), William J. Schultz, *The Taxation of Inheritance*, p. 3 (New York, 1926); and Max West, *The Inheritance Tax*, p. 11 (New York, 1908). *See also, Knowlton v. Moore*, 178 U.S. 41, 49 (1900).

[2] William J. Schultz, *The Taxation of Inheritance*, p. 6 (New York 1926). The Roman death taxes were adopted by Emperor Augustus in 6 A.D. *See also, Max West, The Inheritance Tax*, p. 11 (New York, 1908); and 3 Adam Smith, *The Wealth of Nations*, p. 311 (London, 1811). For a discussion of the complexities of estate planning in ancient Greece, *see, Anton-Herman Chroust, Estate Planning in Hellenic Antiquity: Aristotle's Last Will and Testament,* 45 Notre Dame Lawyer 629 (1969).

[3] The history of using inter vivos transfers to evade death taxes may be traced to Egypt in the seventh century, B.C.. As noted by one author: "Another inscription [Egyptian hieroglyphics] records a sale of property by an old man to his sons at a nominal price, apparently

for the purpose of avoiding the inheritance tax." Max West, The Inheritance Tax, pp. 11-12 (New York, 1908).

4 P.L. 107-16, 107th Cong., 1st Sess. (2001).

5 P.L. 111-312, 111th Cong. 2nd Sess. (2010).

6 For a summary and description of current law in this area, please *see*, CRS Report 95-416, *Federal Estate, Gift, and Generation-Skipping Taxes: A Description of Current Law*, by John R. Luckey.

7 1 *American State Papers in Finance* 277.

8 *Annals of Congress*, 4th Cong., 1st Sess. 993 (1796). The tax proposed by the Ways and means Committee, however, was not graduated, unlike the 1794 recommendation. The Ways and Means proposal called for a flat 2% levy and exempted property passing to parents, husbands, and lineal descendants.

9 Act of July 6, 1797, 1 Stat. 527.

10 The policy of favorable tax treatment of transfers to a spouse has continued into present law, which affords special estate and gift tax deductions for certain interspousal transfers. 26 U.S.C. §§ 2056, and 2523.

11 Act of April 6, 1802, 2 Stat. 148.

12 During consideration of the 1862 tax, Representative William Payne Sheffield of Rhode Island argued unsuccessfully for special treatment of charitable bequests. In debates on the floor of the House of Representatives, Congressman Sheffield stated: It seems to me proper for the national Legislature to give encouragement to making of this class of devises for charitable and literary purposes. There are a great many of them made—made to poor churches and made for the purpose of building schools and colleges. The Government has frequently aided such institutions by grants of land; and it seems to me to be in harmony with the previous policy of our legislature to adopt a provision of this character. *Cong. Globe,* 37th Cong., 2nd Sess. 1534 (1862).

13 Act of July 1, 1862, 12 Stat. 432, 483.

14 An inheritance tax may be distinguished from an estate tax, such as the tax presently imposed by the federal government. An estate tax is imposed upon a decedent's estate for the privilege of passing the property to designated beneficiaries, whereas an inheritance tax is imposed upon the beneficiaries themselves for the privilege of receiving legacies, bequests and devises from the deceased.

15 Act of July 30, 1864, 13 Stat. 285, 480.

16 Act of July 13, 1866, 14 Stat. 140.

17 Act of July 15, 1870, 16 Stat. 256.

25 Act of March 2, 1901, 31 Stat. 946.

26 Act of April 12, 1902, 32 Stat. 96.

27 *See*, quotation in Randolph E. Paul, *Taxation in the United States* p. 88 (Boston, 1954).

28 Act of September 8, 1916, 39 Stat. 756; on rationale for the tax as a revenue measure, *see*, H.Rept. 64-922, 64th Cong., 1st Sess. 1-5 (1916).

29 A gift was presumed to have been made in contemplation of death if it was made within two years of death. The executor could rebut this presumption by showing that the gift was motivated by lifetime considerations, rather than death tax avoidance.

30 256 U.S. 345 (1920).

31 256 U.S. at 348.

32 Act of March 3, 1917, 39 Stat. 1000; for statements regarding its necessity to provide war revenues, *see*, H.Rept. 64- 1366, 64th Cong., 2nd Sess. 1-3 (1917).

33 Act of October 3, 1917, 40 Stat. 300.

34 *See*, H.Rept. 65-767, 65th Cong., 2nd Sess. (1918); and the debates on H.R. 12863, 65th Cong., 2nd Sess., 56 *Cong. Rec.* (1918).

35 Act of February 24, 1919, 40 Stat. 1057.

36 A power of appointment is a right held by someone other than the owner of property, to designate the person or persons who will enjoy the benefits of the property. For example, a power to designate who will receive the income from certain stocks would be a general power of appointment over the income from stocks. The power to designate who would receive the stocks at the owner's death would be a general power of appointment over the stocks themselves.

37 Revenue Act of 1924, Act of June 2, 1924, 43 Stat. 253.

38 Revenue Act of 1926, Act of February 26, 1926, 44 Stat. 9; on the necessity of the estate tax rate increases to provide revenues to finance new Federal projects, *see*, H.Rept. 72-708, 72nd Cong., 1st Sess. 1-4 (1932).

39 280 U.S. 124 (1929).

40 Act of June 6, 1932, 47 Stat. 169.

41 Act of May 10, 1934, 48 Stat. 680.

42 Act of August 30, 1935, 49 Stat. 1014.

43 Act of June 25, 1940, 54 Stat. 516; on the reason for the increased rates, *see*, H.Rept. 76-2491, 76th Cong., 3rd Sess. 1 (1940).

44 Act of September 20, 1941, 55 Stat. 687.

45 Act of October 21, 1942, 56 Stat. 798.

46 Under community property laws, the property acquired by either spouse during their marriage belongs half to each spouse.

47 *See Estate of Eisner v. Comm'r*, B.T.A. Memo. Op. (October 31, 1939); and *Hernandez v. Becker*, 54 F.2d 542 (10th Cir. 1931).

48 Act of April 2, 1948, 62 Stat. 110.

49 26 U.S.C. § 2042. An "incident of ownership" is any economic benefit from the policy, such as the right to change the beneficiary, to borrow against the cash surrender value, or to cancel the policy.

50 P.L. 94-455 §§ 2001-2009; *See also*, Staff on the Joint Committee on Taxation, 94th Cong., 2nd Sess., *General Explanation of the Tax Reform Act of 1976*, 525-597 (1976).

51 P.L. 94-455, 94th Cong., 2nd Sess. (1976).

52 P.L. 94-455 § 2001.

53 P.L. 94-455 § 2001.

54 The credit was a dollar-for-dollar offset against tax, rather than a deduction from the amount of taxable gifts or taxable estate. Therefore, the $47,000 credit was equivalent to an exemption of $175,625 because it would cover the gift or estate tax on a transfer of $175,625.

55 P.L. 94-455 § 2005. This rule never went into effect. Its effective date was suspended and later the rule was repealed retroactively to its date of enactment. See, discussion of the Revenue Act of 1978 and the Crude Oil Windfall Profits Tax Act of 1980, *infra.*

56 P.L. 94-455 § 2002.

57 To further integrate the estate and gift taxes there was an offset in the estate tax marital deduction for gifts which qualify for more than a one-half gift tax marital deduction. To the extent that a decedent's life time taxable interspousal gifts were less than $250,000, the estate tax maximum marital deduction was reduced by the difference between the actual gift tax marital deduction on these transfers and one-half of the value of the gifts. P.L. 94-455 § 2002(a) and (b).

58 P.L. 94-455 § 2001(a)(5).

[59] P.L. 94-455 § 2002(C).
[60] P.L. 94-555, §2003(a).
[61] P.L. 94-455, § 2004(a).
[62] P.L. 94-455 § 2007.
[63] P.L. 94-455 § 2006. This tax never went into effect. Its effective date was suspended, and later it was repealed retroactively to its date of enactment and replaced with a new tax. *See*, P.L. 99-514, §§ 1431-1433.
[64] P.L. 95-600, 95th Cong., 2d Sess. (1978).
[65] P.L. 95-600, § 511(a).
[66] P.L. 96-223, 96th Cong., 2d Sess. (1980).
[67] Executors could elect to use the carryover basis rules on certain estates of decedents who died after December 31, 1976, and before November 7, 1980.
[68] P.L. 97-34, 97th Cong., 1st Sess. (1981); *see also,* H.Rept. 97-201, 97th Cong., 1st Sess. 154-196 (1981); S.Rept. 97- 144, 97th Cong., 1st Sess. 124-142 (1981); and H.Rept. 97-215, 97th Cong., 1st Sess. 247-257 (1981).
[69] P.L. 97-34, § 401. The credit was phased-in as follows:

Year	Credit	Exemption Equivalent
1981	$47,000	$175,625
1982	$62,800	$225,000
1983	$79,300	$275,000
1984	$96,300	$325,000
1985	$121,800	$400,000
1986	$155,800	$500,000
1987+	$192,800	$600,000

[70] P.L. 97-34, § 402.
[71] P.L. 97-34, § 403.
[72] P.L. 97-34, § 403(c).
[73] P.L. 97-34, § 421.
[74] P.L. 97-34, § 422.
[75] P.L. 97-34, § 424(a).
[76] P.L. 97-34, § 441.
[77] P.L. 97-34, § 401(a)(2)(B).
[78] P.L. 97-34, § 426(a).
[79] P.L. 97-34, § 427(a).
[80] P.L. 97-34 § 428.
[81] P.L. 98-369, 98th Cong., 2nd Sess. (1984); *see also*, H.Rept. 98-432, part II, 98th Cong., 2nd Sess. 1504-1522 (1984); S.Rept. 98-169, 98th Cong., 2nd Sess. 711-725 (1984); and H.Rept. 98-861, 98th Cong., 2nd Sess. 774, 1120, and 1235- 1243 (1984).
[82] P.L. 97-448 § 104, 97th Cong., 2nd Sess. (1982), Technical Corrections Act of 1982, included several provisions to clarify the 1981 ERTA Gift and Estate Tax provisions.
[83] P.L. 98-369 § 21.
[84] P.L. 98-369 § 425.
[85] P.L. 98-369 § 1021. Where the stock is indirectly owned and the quantitative requirements are met, an installment payment election may be made, but the 4% interest rate and five-year deferral of principal payments of certain amounts of deferred tax payments, available for directly owned interests, are not applicable.
[86] P.L. 98-369 §§ 1023, 1024.
[87] P.L. 98-369 § 1025.

[88] P.L. 98-369 § 172.

[89] P.L. 98-369 § 1022.

[90] P.L. 98-369 § 525.

[91] P.L. 98-369 § 641.

[92] P.L. 99-514, 99th Cong., 2nd Sess. (1986). *See also*, H.R. Rep. 841, 99th Cong., 2nd Sess. 770-776 (1986).

[93] P.L. 99-514 §§ 1431-1433.

[94] These "direct skips" were not taxed under the 1976 generation-skipping transfer tax.

[95] P.L. 99-514 § 1172.

[96] P.L. 99-514 § 1422.

[97] P.L. 99-514 § 1852(e). This section also makes technical corrections to 26 U.S.C. § 2039 by repealing subsection (c).

[98] P.L. 100-203, 100th Cong., 1st Sess. (1987). *See also*, H.Rept. 100-495, 100th Cong., 1st Sess. 992-998 (1987).

[99] P.L. 100-203, § 10401(a).

[100] This drop in rates was retroactively repealed by P.L. 103-66, § 13208, 103rd Cong., 1st Sess. (1993).

[101] P.L. 100-203, § 10401(b).

[102] P.L. 100-203, § 10411-10413. The retroactive effect of this provision was upheld by the Supreme Court in *U.S. v. Carlton*, 114 S.Ct. 2018 (1994).

[103] P.L. 100-203, § 10402. In general, a freeze transaction involves the division of ownership of a business into two parts, a growth interest and an interest in the current value of the business, which is the interest which is frozen. By selling, at a nominal price, or giving away the growth interest, a taxpayer could maintain control of the business and continue to enjoy the income from the business while excluding any future appreciation in its value from his gross estate. The classic freeze transaction is a recapitalization of a closely held business. The transferor exchanges his common stock for voting preferred stock, which represents the current value of the business entity. New common stock is given to the transferor's children. This stock, at the time of the gift, has practically no value, but as the value of the business appreciates, the appreciation in value is represented in this common stock. If not for this provision, this transaction would "freeze" the transferor's interest in the business at the value it had at the time of the transaction and any appreciation value would pass to his children free of estate taxation because it had been given away. This estate tax benefit is eliminated by treating a retained frozen interest as the equivalent of a retained life estate in the gifted growth interest. This provision was repealed retroactively to the date of its enactment by the Omnibus Reconciliation Act of 1990, P.L. 101-508, § 11601, *supra*.

[104] P.L. 100-647, 100th Cong., 2nd Sess. (1988).

[105] P.L. 100-647, § 1014.

[106] P.L. 100-647, § 3031.

[107] P.L. 100-647, § 5033.

[108] P.L. 100-647, § 6151.

[109] P.L. 100-647, § 1018.

[110] P.L. 101-239, 101st Cong., 1st Sess. (1989).

[111] See, P.L. 101-239, § 7811.

[112] P.L. 101-239, § 7815(d)(1).

[113] P.L. 101-239, § 7515(d)(5).

[114] P.L. 101-239, § 7815(d)(7)(A).

[115] P.L. 101-239, § 7815(d)(7)(B).

[116] P.L. 101-239, § 7815(d)(14).
[117] P.L. 101-239, § 7815(d)(8).
[118] P.L. 101-508, 101st Cong., 2nd Sess. (1990).
[119] See, 26 U.S.C. § 2036.
[120] P.L. 101-508, § 11601.
[121] P.L. 101-508, § 11602.
[122] P.L. 103-66, 103rd Cong., 1st Sess. (1993).
[123] The top rate had dropped to 50% on December 31, 1992.
[124] P.L. 103-66, § 13208.
[125] P.L. 105-34, 105th Cong., 1st Sess. (1997).
[126] P.L. 105-34, § 501. Instead of the code referring to an amount of credit and one having to compute the size of taxable estate which would be covered by that size of credit, the code now sets out the amount of the taxable estate which the unified credit will cover.
[127] *Id.*
[128] P.L. 105-34, § 502.
[129] P.L. 105-34, § 502. The formula for calculating this percentage was included in the section.
[130] P.L. 105-34, § 502. TRA incorporated by reference the definition of "family member" from I.R.C. § 2032A(e)(1), which included the individual's spouse, the individual's ancestors, and the lineal descendants of the individual or his spouse or parent (and the spouses of such lineal descendants).
[131] P.L. 105-34, § 502. Again, TRA utilized the definition of "family member" from I.R.C. § 2032A(e)(1).
[132] P.L. 105-34, § 502. Recapture rules were included if the heirs failed to meet these participation rules.
[133] P.L. 105-34, § 503.
[134] P.L. 105-34, § 506.
[135] P.L. 105-34, § 507.
[136] P.L. 105-34, § 508.
[137] P.L. 105-34, § 511.
[138] P.L. 105-206.
[139] P.L. 105-206 § 6007(b)(1)(A).
[140] P.L. 105-206 § 6007(b)(1)(B).
[141] P.L. 107-16, 107th Cong., 1st Sess. (2001).
[142] P.L. 107-16, § 501. It should be noted that for purposes of compliance with the Congressional Budget Act, P.L. 107- 16, § 901 provided for sunset of its provisions at the end of the year 2010. Therefore, absent congressional action in the interim, the law governing the estate, gift and generation-skipping transfer taxes would revert to the law which was in place on June 7, 2001.
[143] P.L. 107-16, § 511. The 50% rate in 2002 was to be the maximum rate on taxable estates on the portion in excess of $2,500,000. The top rates in succeeding years are to be the maximum rates on taxable estates on the portion in excess of $2,000,000.
[144] P.L. 107-16, § 521. The applicable exclusion amount is a unified amount which can be exempted from the gift and/or estate tax. After the applicable exclusion amount surpassed $1,000,000 in the year 2004, the amount which may be exempted from gifts was limited to $1,000,000, with the remainder of the exempt amount reserved to the taxable estate.
[145] P.L. 107-16, § 531 and § 532. Generally the maximum allowable credit was the lesser of the net tax paid to the State or the statutory ceiling of 26 U.S.C. § 2011(b) (a percentage of the

taxable estate minus $60,000). Many States used the maximum credit allowed under § 2001(b) to constitute the State's estate tax.

[146] P.L. 107-16, § 511(b).

[147] P.L. 107-16, § 521. The family owned business deduction allowed $625,000 in value of qualified family owned business to be deducted from the estate. If an estate opted to use this deduction, the estate was limited to a $675,000 applicable exclusion amount, giving a total of $1,300,000 which was deducted from the estate. Therefore, when the applicable exclusion amount exceeded the $1,300,000 level, it was no longer useful and therefore was repealed.

[148] 26 U.S.C. § 2641.

[149] P.L. 107-16, § 521(c).

[150] P.L. 107-16, § 511(c), see discussion above.

[151] P.L. 107-16, § 511(d).

[152] P.L. 107-16, § 521.

[153] 26 U.S.C. § 1014.

[154] P.L. 107-16, § 541.

[155] P.L. 107-16, § 542.

[156] The applicable exclusion amount and all property passing to the spouse under the unlimited marital deduction would be not subject to the estate tax while still receiving the stepped-up basis and thus avoiding the income tax on the subsequent sale of the property.

[157] P.L. 107-16, § 542. A decedent who is a nonresident not a citizen is limited to a $60,000 step-up.

[158] P.L. 107-16, § 542.

[159] P.L. 107-16, § 542, amending 26 U.S.C. §§ 6018 & 6019.

[160] P.L. 107-16, § 551.

[161] P.L. 107-16, §§ 561 to 563.

[162] P.L. 111-312, 111th Cong. 2nd Sess. (2010).

[163] P.L. 111-312 at § 301(a).

[164] P.L. 111-312 at § 301(b).

[165] P.L. 111-312 at § 301(c).

[166] P.L. 111-312 at § 301(a).

[167] P.L. 111-312 at § 302(c).

[168] P.L. 111-312 at § 302(a)(1).

[169] P.L. 111-312 at § 302(b).

[170] P.L. 111-312 at § 303.

[171] P.L. 111-312 at § 302(a)(2).

[172] P.L. 107-16, § 901.

[173] P.L. 111-312 at § 101(a).

[174] P.L. 111-312 at § 304.

In: Estate and Gift Taxes
Editor: Jacob A. Hughes

ISBN: 978-1-62100-516-2

Chapter 4

FEDERAL ESTATE, GIFT, AND GENERATION-SKIPPING TAXES: A DESCRIPTION OF CURRENT LAW*

John R. Luckey

SUMMARY

This report contains an explanation of the major provisions of the federal estate, gift, and generation-skipping transfer taxes as they apply to transfers in 2011. The discussion provides basic principles to be applied in the computation of these three transfer taxes.

The federal estate and generation-skipping taxes were resurrected by the Tax Relief, Unemployment Insurance Reauthorization, and Job Creation Act of 2010 (P.L. 111-312) after a hiatus of one year (2010). This act also provided elective options for estates of those who died in 2010.

The federal estate tax is computed through a series of adjustments and modifications of a tax base known as the "gross estate." Certain allowable deductions reduce the gross estate to the "taxable estate," to which is then added the total of all lifetime taxable gifts made by the decedent. The tax rates are applied and, after reduction for certain allowable credits, the amount of tax owed by the estate is reached. The top rate for 2011 is 35% and the exclusion amount is $5,000,000.

---

* This is an edited, reformatted and augmented version of a Congressional Research Service publication, CRS Report for Congress 95-416, from www.crs.gov, dated January 19, 2011.

This discussion divides the federal gift tax into two components: the taxable gift and the gift tax computation. The federal gift tax is imposed on lifetime gifts of property. The tax depends in large part upon the fundamental element—the value of the "taxable gift." The taxable gift is determined by reducing the gross value of the gift by the available deductions and exclusions. The gift tax liability determined on the basis of the donor's taxable gifts may be reduced by the unified lifetime credit (which covers the excludible amount of $5,000,000). The annual per donee exclusion is $13,000 ($26,000 for joint gifts) for 2011. The top rate for 2011 is 35%.

The purpose of the generation-skipping transfer tax is to close a perceived loophole in the estate and gift tax system where property could be transferred to successive generations without intervening estate or gift tax consequences. There are two basic forms of generation-skipping transfers; the indirect skip, where the generation one level below the decedent receives some beneficial interest in the property before the property passes to the generation two or more levels below, and the direct skip, where the property passes directly to the generation two or more levels below the decedent. This discussion describes the tax on these types of transfers, its computation and implementation, and use of such concepts as generation assignment and inclusion ratios. The flat rate for this tax in 2011 is 35%.

INTRODUCTION

This report contains an explanation of the major provisions of the federal estate, gift, and generation-skipping transfer taxes as they apply to transfers in 2011. The enactment of the Economic Growth and Tax Relief Reconciliation Act of 2001[1] phased out the estate and generation-skipping taxes over a 10-year period, leaving the gift tax as the only federal transfer tax in 2010. The year 2010 was the first since 1916 in which there was no federal estate tax. There was also a year hiatus for the generation-skipping tax. The Tax Relief, Unemployment Insurance Reauthorization, and Job Creation Act of 2010[2] temporarily (through the end of 2012) reinstated the estate and generation-skipping taxes with lower top rates and larger exemptions and reunified the estate and gift taxes.

The federal estate and gift taxes are unified. This means that these taxes have the same rate structure. There, also, is one lifetime credit which may be applied to these taxes. For 2011 the unified credit covers an applicable amount of $5,000,000.

The federal estate, gift, and generation-skipping tax laws are rather lengthy and complex. This report discusses those major provisions which play the dominant role in the determination of estate, gift, and generation-skipping tax liability. The discussion relates only to the taxation of United States citizens and resident aliens. Different rules apply to the taxation of nonresident alien individuals.

THE FEDERAL ESTATE TAX

The federal estate tax is a tax on the estate of a decedent, levied against and paid by the estate, as opposed to an inheritance tax which is imposed on and paid by the heirs of the decedent based upon what they receive. The federal estate tax is computed through a series of adjustments and modifications of a tax base known as the "gross estate." Certain allowable deductions reduce the gross estate to the "taxable estate," to which is then added the total of all lifetime taxable gifts made by the decedent. The tax rates are then applied. The result is the decedent's estate tax which, after reduction for certain allowable credits, is the amount of tax paid by the estate. This discussion will divide the federal estate tax into three components: the gross estate, deductions from the gross estate, and computation of the tax, including allowable tax credits.

The Gross Estate: The Federal Estate Tax Base

The gross estate of a deceased individual includes both property owned by the decedent on the date of the decedent's death and certain interests in property which the decedent had transferred to another person at some time prior to the date of death. The conditions under which such property and interests in property may be included in the decedent's gross estate often constitute an important problem area in the administration of the estate tax laws.

The gross estate of a decedent includes the value of all property, real or personal, tangible or intangible, wherever situated, in which the deceased owned an interest on the date of the decedent's death.[3] The property and interests in property included in the decedent's gross estate are valued at their fair market value on the date of death or, if elected by the executor, the alternate valuation date. The alternate valuation date is the earlier of the date of distribution or disposition of the property by the estate or the date six months after the date of death.[4] The "fair market value" of property is normally described as the price at which a willing buyer would purchase the property and a willing seller would sell it, both being fully informed as to all relevant facts. It is, consequently, the value of the property at its "highest and best use," rather than its current use.[5] There is, however, a special rule under which the real estate used in certain family farms and closely held businesses will, under certain conditions, be valued for estate tax purposes at less than its highest and best use.[6]

Certain types of property are included in a decedent's gross estate under special rules. The proceeds from a life insurance policy on the life of the deceased will be included in the decedent's gross estate if either the proceeds are payable to or for the use of the executor or the estate, or if the decedent held any "incidents of ownership" in the policy on the date of death or gave away such incidents of ownership within three years of the date of death.[7] An incident of ownership is an economic right in the policy, such as the right to cancel the policy, change the beneficiary, or borrow against its cash surrender value. The value of a survivor's annuity payable because of the death of the decedent will be included in the decedent's gross estate if the deceased had the right to receive a lifetime annuity under the same contract.[8]

The value of property owned by the decedent jointly with a right of survivorship in another person, other than the decedent's spouse, is fully included in the decedent's gross estate, except to the extent it can be shown that someone other than the decedent contributed money or money's worth of consideration towards the cost of acquiring the property.[9] Only one-half of the value of property owned jointly with a right of survivorship by a decedent and the surviving spouse will be included in the decedent's gross estate, regardless of the relative contributions of the decedent and the surviving spouse.[10]

In a number of instances, the value of a decedent's gross estate includes the value of property not owned by the decedent on the date of death. A decedent's gross estate includes the value of lifetime gifts over which the decedent retained a life interest[11] or a power to alter, amend, terminate, or destroy the beneficial enjoyment of the property.[12] The value of lifetime gifts which are not to take effect until the date of death are also included in the donor's gross estate.[13] The gross estate includes the value of these types of property which have been transferred, irrespective of the number of years which have elapsed between the date of the gift and the date of the donor's death. The value of property sold during the decedent's lifetime, for full and adequate consideration in money or money's worth, is not included in the decedent's gross estate under these sections of the Internal Revenue Code.

The gross estate also includes the value of interests in property given away within three years of the date of death if, had the property been retained, it would have been included in the decedent's gross estate under one of the three special rules noted above or under special rules for life insurance proceeds. Property given away within three years of the date of death is also included in the decedent's gross estate for purposes of qualifying for certain estate and income tax benefits.[14]

The value of all property subject to a general power of appointment held by the decedent on the date of death will be included in the decedent's gross estate, even if the decedent died without exercising the power. A power of appointment is a right, held by a person other than the owner of property, to determine who will enjoy the ownership of or benefit of the property. A power of appointment is "general" if it may be exercised by its holder in favor of the holder, the holder's estate, the holder's creditors, or the creditors of the holder's estate. If a power cannot be exercised in favor of these classes of persons, it is not a general power of appointment, regardless of the size of the classes of beneficiaries in whose favor the power can be exercised.[15]

Deductions from the Gross Estate: Reaching the Taxable Estate

A decedent's taxable estate is determined by reducing the gross estate by allowable deductions, including estate administration expenses, certain debts and losses, the amount of qualified transfers to a surviving spouse, charitable bequests, and State death taxes.

The first deduction to which an estate is entitled is for the funeral expenses, administration expenses, claims against the estate, and unpaid mortgages paid by the estate (to the extent not reflected in the reduced value of estate assets). These payments may be deducted to the extent that they are paid by the estate and to the extent they are allowable under the laws of the applicable jurisdiction in which the estate is administered.[16] Additionally, the estate may deduct the amount of any casualty or theft losses sustained by the estate during settlement, to the extent such losses are not compensated by insurance.[17]

The estate is also entitled to a "marital deduction" for the value of all property passing to the decedent's surviving spouse.[18] Interests which may terminate in favor of another person upon the lapse of time, the occurrence of an event or contingency, or the failure of an event or contingency to occur, generally do not qualify for the estate tax marital deduction.[19] The estate tax marital deduction is allowed only for non-terminable interests passing to the surviving spouse. These interests may pass to the spouse under the terms of the decedent's will, by law of intestacy, by contract, by operation of law, or otherwise. Special exceptions to the terminable interest rule are made for certain transfers in trust of a lifetime income interest if the executor elects to include the value of the trust property in the surviving spouse's gross estate, and for certain life estates coupled with a general power of appointment, as well as for certain life insurance settlement options and certain interests conditioned upon survivorship for a reasonable period not exceeding six months.[20]

The gross estate is also reduced by the value of certain charitable bequests and devises to qualified charitable organizations.[21] An estate tax deduction is generally permitted for any transfer which, if made during the decedent's lifetime would have been deductible for income tax purposes, though the rules are not identical.[22]

The gross estate is also reduced by the amount of any estate, inheritance, legacy, or succession taxes actually paid to any State or the District of Columbia in respect to property included in the gross estate.[23]

Computation of the Estate Tax Liability

Under the unified estate and gift tax system, computation of a decedent's estate tax liability requires a grossed-up, a combining, of the decedent's lifetime taxable gifts and the decedent's taxable estate to which the tax rate schedule is applied. Then, any available credits are taken to obtain the decedent's actual estate tax liability.[24]

The estate rate schedule[25] is as follows:

Taxable Estate	Tentative Tax
not over $10,000	18% of such amount
$10,000-$20,000	$1,800 + 20% of excess over $10,000
$20,000-$40,000	$3,800 + 22% of excess over $20,000
$40,000-$60,000	$8,200 + 24% of excess over $40,000

Taxable Estate	Tentative Tax
$60,000-$80,000	$13,000 + 26% of excess over $60,000
$80,000-$100,000	$18,200 + 28% of excess over $80,000
$100,000-$150,000	$23,800 + 30% of excess over $100,000
$150,000-$250,000	$38,800 + 32% of excess over $150,000
$250,000-$500,000	$70,800 + 34% of excess over $250,000
$500,000 +	35% of excess over $500,000

There are three major estate tax credits presently in effect: the unified transfer tax credit, the credit for foreign death taxes, and the credit for federal estate taxes paid by previous estates. Each credit is a dollar-for-dollar offset against an estate's federal estate tax liability.

The unified tax credit is available against both lifetime gift tax liabilities and the estate tax liability. To the extent this credit is used to offset gift taxes, it is unavailable to offset estate taxes. The credit is expressed in the code as an "applicable exclusion amount," that is, the amount of taxable gifts or estate that the credit would cover. The applicable exclusion amount in 2011 is $5,000,000.[26] A surviving spouse may also use any unused applicable exclusion amount of their spouse.[27]

Each estate is also allowed credits for foreign death taxes, including estate, inheritance, legacy, or succession taxes actually paid by the estate or any heir with respect to property included in the federal gross estate. This credit is limited to the amount of U.S. estate taxes paid on the same property. The credit is computed as the same proportionate share of the total U.S. estate taxes as the value of the foreign taxed property bears to the total of the U.S. taxable estate.[28]

The credit for previously taxed property (the PTP credit) is provided to relieve some of the harshness that could otherwise result when an individual dies soon after inheriting property upon which a federal estate tax has already been imposed. The PTP credit is allowed for all or some portion of the federal estate taxes paid on property transferred to the decedent within the past ten years. The PTP credit is graduated according to the amount of time that has elapsed between the date the property was transferred to the decedent and the date of death. The maximum PTP credit is 100% of the previously paid taxes, when the decedent received the property within the first two years prior to the date of death. The minimum PTP credit is 20% of the previously paid taxes, when the decedent received the property during the ninth or tenth years preceding the date of death.[29]

The Federal Gift Tax

The federal gift tax is imposed on lifetime gifts of property.[30] The tax depends in large part upon the fundamental element—the value of the "taxable gift." The taxable gift is determined by reducing the gross value of the gift by the available deductions and exclusions. The gift tax liability determined on the basis of the donor's taxable gifts may be reduced by the available unified transfer tax credit.

The Taxable Gift

Determining the amount of a taxable gift is fundamental to determining the donor's ultimate gift tax liability. The amount of the taxable gift is the fair market value of the gift at the time it was made, less certain exclusions and deductions.[31] The major deductions and exclusions are the annual per donee exclusion, the gift tax marital deduction, and the gift tax charitable deduction.

Every donor may exclude from the federal gift tax base the first $13,000 of cash or property given to each donee annually.[32] An unlimited exclusion is available for gifts made by paying an individual's tuition or medical expenses. The annual exclusion is unavailable, however, for gifts of future interests which vest in the donee only upon some future date. The present interest rule often requires complicated drafting techniques to obtain the annual exclusion for the value of a gift of a life insurance policy made in trust, or a gift to a minor, to be held in trust until the minor reaches a certain age.[33]

Married couples may double the annual exclusion through "gift-splitting," an arrangement in which one spouse consents to being treated as having made one-half of the gifts made by his or her spouse in that taxable year.[34] The election is made by a notation on the gift tax return, and results in each spouse receiving a $13,000 per donee exclusion for one-half of the value of the same gift. Therefore, married couples may annually exclude $26,000 per donee from tax by gift-splitting.

A deduction is also allowed for all of the value of certain interspousal gifts.[35] Like its estate tax counterpart, no gift tax marital deduction is allowed for most gifts of terminable interests.[36]

A donor may also deduct the value of certain charitable gifts. The value of the gift may be deducted only if the charity is of a type described in the applicable statutory provision, which describes most, but not all, of the charities for which deductible income tax contributions may be made.[37]

The division of property incident to a divorce or separation agreement may result in the interspousal transfer of property for a consideration which is not adequate for gift tax purposes. Consequently, the Code provides that interspousal transfers pursuant to a written agreement dividing the property of the spouses and occurring within two years before and one year after a decree of divorce will not be treated as taxable gifts, as long as the marital rights of the spouses are settled by the agreement or it provides for a reasonable allowance for the support of minor children.[38]

The renunciation of property given one by another person might be viewed as either the negation of the initial gift, resulting in no gift tax liability, or as a reciprocal gift, resulting in two gift tax liabilities. If a disclaimer is made in writing, before the donee has accepted any benefits of the property, and within nine months of the date the gift was made, the gift will be ignored for gift tax purposes.[39]

The Gift Tax Computation

The tax on a taxable gift is measured initially by the value of the transferred property, and is cumulative in nature.[40] The applicable rate of tax on a taxable gift is determined by the total of the donor's lifetime taxable gifts The estate and gift tax rate tables are identical.[41]

The actual computation of the gift tax for each calendar year is completed in three steps. First, the donor's taxable gifts for the calendar year and any preceding calendar periods are totaled and the tentative tax determined. Second, the tentative tax is calculated on the total taxable gifts for preceding calendar periods. Third, the result from step two is subtracted from the result of step one, and the donor's unused unified tax credit is applied to the remaining amount.[42]

THE TAX ON GENERATION-SKIPPING TRANSFERS

The Tax Reform Act of 1986 repealed the generation-skipping transfer tax, enacted in 1976, as being unduly complicated and replaced it with a simplified flat-rate tax.[43] The purpose of the resulting generation-skipping transfer tax is the same as predecessor, to close a loophole in the estate and gift tax system where property could be transferred to successive generations without paying multiple estate or gift taxes. The traditional generation-skipping transfers were trusts established by a parent for the life time benefit of the children with the remainder passing to the grandchildren. If properly drafted, no estate or gift tax would be imposed when the trust corpus passed from the settlor's children to the settlor's grandchildren because the estate tax is not imposed on interests which terminate at death.

There are two basic forms of generation-skipping transfers; the indirect skip, where the generation one level below the decedent (e.g., children) receives some beneficial interest in the property before the property passes to the generation two or more levels below (e.g., grandchildren), and the direct skip, where the property passes directly to the generation two or more levels below the decedent (e.g., grandchildren). The 1976 law only taxed the indirect skip. The current system taxes both types of transfers.

The generation-skipping tax is a flat-rate tax. The rate is set at the highest estate tax rate, currently 35%.[44] This tax rate is applied to three different events, a taxable distribution, a taxable termination, or a direct skip.

A taxable distribution is a distribution from a trust, other than a taxable termination or direct skip, to a skip person.[45] A skip person is a person assigned to a generation two or more generations below the transferor's.[46]

A taxable termination is a termination by death, lapse of time, release of power, or otherwise of an interest in property held in trust, unless immediately after the termination a non-skip person has an interest in the property or at no time after the termination may a distribution be made from the trust to a skip person.[47]

A direct skip is a transfer to a skip person. A transfer to a trust is a direct skip if all the interests in the trust are held by skip persons.[48]

All persons are assigned a generation level under the statute. Persons related to the transferor or spouse are assigned along family lines. For example, the transferor, spouse, and brothers and sisters are in one generation, their children in the next and grandchildren the next. Lineal descendants of a grandparent of the transferor or spouse are assigned to generations on the same basis. Anyone ever married to a lineal descendant of the transferor's grandparent or the spouse's grandparent are assigned to the level of their spouse who was a lineal descendant. Non-relatives of the transferor are assigned generations measured from the birth of the transferor. Persons not more than 121/2 years younger are treated as members of the same generation as the transferor. Each 25-year period thereafter is treated as a new generation. A grandchild of the transferor or spouse is moved up one generation if his parents are deceased at the time of the transfer.[49]

Several exemptions or exclusions are provided in the statutory scheme.[50] The exclusions for tuition and medical expense payments from the gift tax[51] also apply to the generation-skipping tax.[52] The $13,000 per donee annual exclusion from the gift tax is recognized against taxation of direct skips only (i.e., where the property passes directly to the generation two or more levels below the decedent).[53] A $5,000,000 GST exemption is allowed to each individual for generation-skipping transfers during life or at death.[54] Again, the exemption is doubled for married individuals who elect to treat the transfers as made one-half by each.[55]

The GST exemption may be allocated by the transferor or the executor to any generation-skipping transfer. Once the allocation is made it is irrevocable. Unless a contrary election is made, all or any portion of the exclusion not previously allocated is deemed allocated to a lifetime direct skip to the extent necessary to make the inclusion ratio for the transfer zero.[56]

The inclusion ratio is figured by subtracting from one a fraction, the numerator of which is the portion of the GST exemption allocated to the transfer, the denominator of which is the value of the property transferred.[57] To compute the generation-skipping tax, the value of the transfer is multiplied by the tax rate (35%) and by the inclusion ratio.[58]

The liability for the tax is determined by the type of transfer. In the case of a taxable distribution, the tax is paid by the transferee. The tax on taxable terminations or direct skips from a trust is paid by the trustee. Direct skips, other than those from a trust, are taxed to the transferor.[59]

ELECTIONS AVAILABLE TO ESTATES OF INDIVIDUALS WHO DIED IN 2010

The year 2010 was the first since 1916 in which there was no federal estate tax, but heirs of decedents who died in 2010 were subject to carry-over basis in inherited property. There was also a year hiatus for the generation-skipping tax. The Tax Relief, Unemployment Insurance Reauthorization, and Job Creation Act of 2010[60] temporarily (through the end of 2012) reinstated the estate and generation-skipping taxes with lower top rates and larger exemptions, reunified the estate and gift taxes, and reinstituted stepped-up basis rules (discussed below) for property received from a decedent. The act provided for an election for 2010 estates to either use the carryover basis rules which were in effect in 2010 or opt to have the reinstated estate tax regimen apply to the estate, with the benefit of the stepped-up basis rules. Which option is more beneficial depends on the size of the estate, whether the assets are to be sold, and the nature and basis of the property in the estate.

Technically, basis rules are income tax rules, not estate tax rules. Basis is used to determine gain on the sale of capital assets for income tax purposes. Often basis and cost are equivalent. Generally, to determine taxable income from sale of a capital asset, the basis in that asset is subtracted from the sale price. Prior to 2010 and currently the basis in property received from a decedent was/is a "stepped-up" basis.[61] The inheritor of property, instead of having the basis of the one from whom he received the property (a carry-over basis), has a basis in the property of its fair market value at the date of death of the decedent. The purpose of the stepped-up basis rule is to avoid double taxation. The property has been subject to the estate tax. If the property had a carry-over basis and was sold after inheritance, there would be a capital gain subject to the income tax. The use of the stepped-up basis eliminates this capital gain and thus the income tax on the sale.

In 2010 there was no federal estate tax. Therefore, there was no chance of this type of double taxation and thus this need for the stepped-up basis rules was removed. In 2010 the basis in property received from a decedent was the lesser of carry-over basis or the fair market value of the property on the date of death of the decedent.[62] Under the estate tax and the income tax stepped-up basis rules, an amount of the gross estate was not subject to either tax.[63] To avoid penalizing decedents with estates below the estate tax threshold (whose property would have otherwise received a carry-over basis), two amounts of property received from a decedent still received stepped-up basis. Every estate could allocate $1,300,000 basis increase to property in the estate.[64] In addition to this general step-up, property which passed to the spouse of the decedent could be allocated up to $3,000,000 basis increase.[65]

End Notes

[1] P.L. 107-16, 107th Cong., 1st Sess. (2001).

[2] P.L. 111-312, 111th Cong. 2nd Sess. (2010).

[3] 26 U.S.C. § 2031(a).

[4] 26 U.S.C. § 2032(a). The alternate valuation date is useful when the value of the property contained in the gross estate has decreased following the death of the decedent, such as

might be the case when the estate holds a substantial quantity of stock in a corporation in which the decedent was a dominant figure.

[5] Treas. Regs. (26 C.F.R.) § 20.2031-1(b).

[6] 26 U.S.C. § 2032A. An election for special use valuation may be made by the executor where the majority of the estate is made up of closely-held business property. Under this election the executor may choose to value the property at its closely-held business value rather than its value at its highest and best use. The special use valuation cannot, however, reduce the gross estate by more than $1,020,000 in 2011 (This limit is indexed for inflation each year).

[7] 26 U.S.C. § 2042.

[8] 26 U.S.C. § 2039(a). Annuities are valued according to the actuarial life expectancy of the annuitant, the frequency of the payments, and the size of the payments. Treas. Regs. Sec. 20.2039-1.

[9] 26 U.S.C. § 2040(a).

[10] 26 U.S.C. 2040(b).

[11] 26 U.S.C. § 2036. The retention of an estate, the duration of which is not ascertainable except with reference to the lifetime of the donor, is also treated as a retained life interest, as is the retention of the right to vote the stock of certain closely-held corporations. 26 U.S.C. § 2036(b); *see also, United States v. Byrum*, 408 U.S. 125 (1972).

[12] 26 U.S.C. § 2038. These transfers are also known as "revocable transfers" because the retained power allowed the deceased donor to revoke the transfer and return to himself or herself the enjoyment of the transferred property.

[13] 26 U.S.C. § 2037.

[14] 26 U.S.C. § 2035.

[15] 26 U.S.C. § 2041. Certain other powers are statutorily classified as limited or non-special powers of appointment, including the right to invade the corpus (principal) subject to the power, only under an ascertainable standard relating to health, education, support or maintenance, or the non-cumulative right to withdraw up to the greater of $5,000 or 5% of corpus annually.

[16] 26 U.S.C. § 2053.

[17] 26 U.S.C. § 2054.

[18] 26 U.S.C. § 2056.

[19] 26 U.S.C. § 2056(b). Generally, the unlimited marital deduction is not allowed for transfers to a surviving spouse who is not a citizen of the United States and does not become a citizen before the estate tax return is filed unless the transfer utilizes a qualified domestic trust. See 26 U.S.C. § 2056(d). A qualified domestic trust is defined in 26 U.S.C. § 2056A to be a trust which has at least one trustee who is a United States citizen and which citizen trustee has veto power over distributions from the trust.

[20] 26 U.S.C. § 2056(b).

[21] 26 U.S.C. § 2055.

[22] *Compare*, 26 U.S.C. §§ 2055(a) and 170(c).

[23] 26 U.S.C. § 2058.

[24] 26 U.S.C. § 2001(b).

[25] 26 U.S.C. § 2001(c). Because of the applicable exclusion amount of $5,000,000, estates which actually pay the federal estate tax have basically a flat rate of 35%.

[26] 26 U.S.C. § 2010.

[27] 26 U.S.C. § 2010(c).

[28] 26 U.S.C. § 2014.

[29] 26 U.S.C. § 2013.

[30] The word "gift" is not defined in the tax laws, but the Code does state that the amount of a gift is ascertained when "property is transferred for less than an adequate and full consideration in money or money's worth," 26 U.S.C. § 2512(b). Generally, the regulations state that a gift is made, for gift tax purposes, when there is a transfer for inadequate consideration and the transaction does not take place in a business context. Treas. Regs. § 25.2511. This should be distinguished from the definition of a "gift" for income tax purposes, which requires that the transfer be made from "detached and disinterested generosity." *Comm'r v. Duberstein*, 363 U.S. 278 (1960). A transfer may, therefore, be a gift for gift tax purposes, because there was no legally sufficient consideration, but not constitute a gift for income tax purposes, because it was not motivated by detached and disinterested generosity.

[31] 26 U.S.C. § 2512. Special valuation rules for valuation freezing transactions are set forth in 26 U.S.C. § 2701 through 2704.

[32] 26 U.S.C. § 2503. This figure is indexed for inflation.

[33] But see 26 U.S.C. § 2503(c), for a special rule granting the annual exclusion for gifts to certain trusts created for the benefit of minors which permit the income to be expended for the benefit of the minor until the minor attains age 21, and requires the minor to be given outright ownership of the trust assets at that age or, if the minor should die prior to attaining age 21, to designate by will or otherwise the disposition of the property.

[34] 26 U.S.C. § 2513. Gift-splitting also permits use of both spouses' unified transfer tax credits to eliminate present tax on lifetime taxable gifts.

[35] 26 U.S.C. § 2523(a).

[36] 26 U.S.C. § 2523(b),(f).

[37] 26 U.S.C. § 2522, *compare*, 26 U.S.C. § 170(c).

[38] 26 U.S.C. § 2516.

[39] 26 U.S.C. § 2518.

[40] 26 U.S.C. § 2501.

[41] 26 U.S.C. § 2001(c).

[42] 26 U.S.C. §§ 2502, 2001(c), 2505. P.L. 111-312 restored the total unification of the unified credit so that the full applicable exclusion amount is available to offset gifts. The 35% top rate must be used for computing the amount of credit used when grossing up any previously made gifts where a higher rate was used.

[43] Staff of the Joint Committee on Taxation, 100th Cong., 1st Sess., *General Explanation of the Tax Reform Act of 1986*, 1263 (1987). P.L. 11-312 brought back the generation-skipping transfer tax after a hiatus for 2010.

[44] 26 U.S.C. § 2641(a).

[45] 26 U.S.C. § 2612.

[46] 26 U.S.C. § 2613.

[47] 26 U.S.C. § 2612.

[48] 26 U.S.C. § 2612.

[49] 26 U.S.C. § 2651.

[50] P.L. 99-514, § 1433(b)(3) provided that for transfers made prior to January 1, 1990, each grantor could exempt $2,000,000 in direct skips per grandchild ($4,000,000 for married individuals who elect to treat the transfers as made one-half by each).

[51] 26 U.S.C. § 2503.

[52] 26 U.S.C. § 2611(b).

[53] 26 U.S.C. § 2642(c).

[54] 26 U.S.C. § 2631. The GST exemption is to be equal to the estate tax applicable exclusion amount.

[55] 26 U.S.C. § 2652.
[56] 26 U.S.C. § 2632.
[57] 26 U.S.C. § 2642.
[58] 26 U.S.C. § 2641.
[59] 26 U.S.C. § 2603.
[60] P.L. 111-312, 111th Cong. 2nd Sess. (2010).
[61] 26 U.S.C. § 1014.
[62] P.L. 107-16, § 542.
[63] The applicable exclusion amount and all property passing to the spouse under the unlimited marital deduction would not be subject to the estate tax while still receiving the stepped-up basis and thus avoiding the income tax on the subsequent sale of the property.
[64] P.L. 107-16, § 542. A decedent who is a nonresident and not a citizen is limited to a $60,000 step-up.
[65] P.L. 107-16, § 542.

In: Estate and Gift Taxes
Editor: Jacob A. Hughes

ISBN: 978-1-62100-516-2

Chapter 5

ASSET DISTRIBUTION OF TAXABLE ESTATES: AN ANALYSIS*

Steven Maguire

SUMMARY

This report provides data on the distribution of assets in estates as reported on estate tax returns filed in 2009. This report finds that farm and business assets represent a small share of the total value of taxable estates that filed tax returns in 2009, (3.25% and 13.86%, respectively). That share is concentrated in estates valued over $10 million.

INTRODUCTION

The estate and gift tax debate focuses on issues of equity and long-term economic efficiency. Following is a brief of the two sides of the debate. Many observers opposed to the estate tax on grounds of equity suggest that taxing the assets of decedents is unfair because the decedent has already paid taxes on the assets as they accumulated value. There is also a perceived need to provide heirs of family farms and businesses a tax preference for family assets that are

* This is an edited, reformatted and augmented version of a Congressional Research Service publication, CRS Report for Congress RS20593, from www.crs.gov, dated January 21, 2011.

transferred at death. Opponents of the estate tax on economic efficiency grounds cite research that suggests the estate tax is a tax on saving and investment, which, like other taxes on capital, would tend to impede long-term economic growth.[1]

Those in favor of retaining some type of estate tax counter that many estates include assets with accumulated capital gains that have not been subject to income taxes. For example, publicly traded stock transferred at death would avoid taxation on the increased value from the time of purchase to the date of transfer.[2] Estate tax proponents maintain that other assets, such as family business assets and family farm assets, should not be afforded special preferences in the tax code.[3]

Repeal or modification of the estate and gift tax for all estates would achieve the policy objective of tax relief for farm and small-business estates. However, farm assets and business assets represent a relatively small share of total taxable estate value, approximately 17.1% of gross taxable estate value in 2009. Thus, repeal or modification of the estate tax would benefit more estates with a variety of different asset types.

Examining the asset distribution of estates that paid at least some estate tax more closely will provide some guidance for policy makers about the current impact of estate taxes on business-type assets and farms. The Internal Revenue Service (IRS) annually publishes data on the distribution of assets in estate tax returns filed in a tax year. This report uses data for returns filed in 2009.

Note, however, the year the return is filed does not always correspond to the year of death as the estate has nine months from date of death to file a return. For example, data from returns filed in 2009 includes the returns of many decedents who died in 2008. The biggest difference between 2008 and 2009 is the exemption amount, which was $2 million in 2008 and rose to $3.5 million in 2009. For 2011 and 2012, the exemption amount is $5 million ($10 million for married decedents). The current status of estate tax law is reviewed in the next section and is followed by a presentation of the 2009 IRS data.

Recent Legislative Activity and Overview

On December 17, 2010, the *Tax Relief, Unemployment Insurance Reauthorization, and Job Creation Act of 2010* (P.L. 111-312) reinstated the estate tax beginning with 2010 decedents and sunsets after 2012, reverting to the estate tax law in place before EGTRRA. The new law sets the estate tax exemption level at $5 million per decedent in 2010 (indexed for inflation) and establishes a top marginal tax rate of 35%. Any unused exemption amount is transferrable to a surviving spouse yielding an effective exemption amount of $10 million for married decedents.

The Joint Committee on Taxation estimates the temporary estate tax modifications to reduce revenue by approximately $136.7 billion over 10 years.[4] The number of decedents that will be affected by the estate tax will rise significantly in 2013 as the law will return to the pre-EGTRRA parameters.

The estate and gift tax minimum filing requirement is $5 million for deaths occurring in 2010. Executors of estates in 2010 may also choose to file under the EGTRRA laws in place before passage of P.L. 111-312. Generally, estates valued below the threshold are not required to file a return. Estates valued over the threshold amount calculate their tax liability based upon the entire (or gross) value of the estate inclusive of the $5 million. Deductions from the gross estate value, such as bequests to a surviving spouse (the marital deduction), state estate and inheritance taxes, and donations to charitable organizations, are then subtracted from the gross estate value. The tentative tax liability is determined by the progressive rate schedule provided for in the tax code.

The next step in the calculation of estate tax liability, and perhaps the most important, is the applicable credit. The applicable credit is set such that an estate has the equivalent of a $5 million exemption (for deaths occurring in 2010, see Table 1 below). In many cases, the marital deduction combined with the deduction for charitable contributions can eliminate all estate tax liability.

Table 1. Increases in the Filing Requirement

Year of Death	Filing Requirement or Equivalent Exemption	Applicable Credit
2009	$3,500,000	$1,525,800
2010	estate tax repealed with carryover basis or $5 million exemption with stepped-up basis	
2011	$5,000,000 + inflation adjustment	
2012	$5,000,000 + inflation adjustment	
2013 and after	$1,000,000 $	1,000,000

Before 2005, estates were allowed to claim a credit for state death taxes paid. EGTRRA, however, gradually repealed the credit for state death taxes; eliminating it in 2005 and replacing it with a deduction for taxes paid. Many states have relied on the federal credit for their estate tax and will need to modify their tax laws to continue collecting their estate and inheritance taxes.

According to a April 2009 evaluation of state laws by the Center on Budget and Policy Priorities, "Some 22 states—continue to collect either an estate or inheritance tax."[5]

The data utilized in this report are from the Internal Revenue Service (IRS), Statistics of Income (SOI) Division.[6] The SOI data report the assets held by estates by gross estate value classes. For this report, farm returns are defined as estates reporting farm assets. Business returns are defined as those estates that include assets typically held by businesses: "closely held stock," "limited partnerships," "real estate partnerships," and "other non-corporate business assets." Estates reporting one or more of the four assets were termed business returns. This methodology is imperfect and likely double counts many estates. As a result, the number of business estates would be significantly *overstated* by this estimate.

TAXABLE ESTATE TAX RETURNS

Of the approximately 2.43 million deaths in 2008 of people 25 years old and over, 0.6% incurred estate and gift tax liability.[7] Further, only 1,846 decedents with taxable estates included farm assets (0.08% of all deaths), and 8,055 taxable estates listed assets of the type typically held by businesses (0.34% of all deaths). The primary reason for the low number of filers relative to the number of deaths in 2008 is the high gross estate value filing threshold. In tax year 2008, only estates valued at greater than $2,000,000 were required to file an estate and gift tax return.[8] (The 2008 decedents would likely file returns in 2009.) This makes the estate tax a relatively progressive tax source.

Table 2 suggests the progressivity of the estate and gift tax in 2009. Taxable estates worth over $10 million accounted for 11.2% of the total taxable estates, yet 61.0% of all estate tax revenue. The 4,296 estates (29.2% of taxable estates) larger than $5 million generated over 81.9% of total estate tax revenue. Recall that only 0.7% of deaths generated any estate tax liability.

Table 2. Wealth Distribution of Taxable Returns Filed in 2009

Size of Gross Estate	Taxable Returns	Gross Taxable Estate Value ($ in thousands)	Net Estate Tax ($ in thousands)	Percent of Taxable Estate Returns	Percent Federal Net Estate Tax Revenue
All Returns	14,713	101,971,360	20,643,664	100.0%	100.0%
Under 2.0 million[a]	555	883,347	68,894	3.8%	0.3%

Source: Internal Revenue Service, Statistics of Income Division, September 2010, *Estate Tax Returns Filed in 2009, by Tax Status and Size of Gross Estate*.

[a] In 2009, most tax returns were filed for deaths occurring in 2008, for which the estate tax exemption level was $2 million. However, due to filing extensions, a limited number of returns were filed in 2009 for deaths occurring prior to 2007, when the filing threshold would have been below $2 million.

Asset Distribution of Taxable Estates

The SOI data do not distinguish estate tax returns by detailed occupation of the decedent, such as farmer or business person. However, the data do provide significant detail on the distribution of the decedent's assets. Table 3 summarizes estate tax return asset data from the returns filed in 2009. Generally, assets that represent more of the taxable estate shoulder a greater share of the tax burden. The value of taxable estates is concentrated in the following asset categories: publicly traded stock, cash assets, state and local bonds, other real estate, and closely held stock. These five assets represent 66.2% of total taxable estate value in 2009. Thus, eliminating the estate tax will reduce the tax burden on these assets.

Farm and Business Assets

Table 3 reports that the value of total farm assets is approximately 3.25% of total taxable gross estate value. The business assets in Table 3 represent approximately $14.1 billion of total taxable estate value (or 13.9%). The largest is closely held stock, worth approximately $7.2 billion. However, total business assets as reported do not explicitly indicate the portion of those assets held in small businesses.

Table 3. Asset Distribution of Taxable Estate Tax Returns Filed in 2009

IRS Defined Asset Category	Total Asset Value ($ in thousands)	Percent of Total Taxable Estate Value
Gross estate	101,971,360	100.00%
Publicly traded stock	25,923,098	25.42%
Cash assets	12,628,073	12.38%
State and local bonds	11,386,174	11.17%
Other real estate	10,402,655	10.20%
Closely held stocka	7,163,259	7.02%
Personal residence	6,282,426	6.16%
Retirement assets	4,911,240	4.82%
Farm assetsa	3,314,559	3.25%
Other Federal bonds	2,745,389	2.69%
Mortgages and notes	2,581,174	2.53%
Real estate partnershipsa	2,459,476	2.41%
Other limited partnershipsa	2,425,733	2.38%
Other noncorporate business assets[a]	2,083,579	2.04%
Art	1,677,971	1.65%
Insurance, face value	1,248,168	1.22%
Corporate and foreign bonds	1,203,884	1.18%
Other assets	1,197,485	1.17%
Private equity and hedge funds	869,063	0.85%
Unclassifiable mutual funds	728,393	0.71%
Depletables / intangibles	413,262	0.41%
Bond funds	250,620	0.25%
Federal savings bonds	125,241	0.12%
Insurance, policy loans	49,558	0.05%

Source: Internal Revenue Service, Statistics of Income Division, September 2010, *Estate Tax Returns Filed in 2009, by Tax Status and Size of Gross Estate*.

[a] Indicates an asset that is included in this report's definition of a business estate.

Table 4. Percent of Taxable Estates Filed in 2009 with Farm Assets and Business Assets by Size of Estate

	Taxable Estate Value ($ in thousands)			Percent of Taxable Estate Value in Class Represented	
Size of Gross Estate	Gross	Farm Assets	Business Assets	Farm Assets	Business Assets
All Returns	101,971,360	3,314,559	14,132,047	3.25%	13.86%
Under 2.0 million[a]	883,347	46,950[b]	34,880	5.32%	3.95%
2.0 to 3.5 million	18,555,977	927,655	789,964	5.00%	4.26%
3.5 to 5.0 million	11,873,398	306,836	615,064	2.58%	5.18%
5.0 to 10.0 million	18,066,733	618,353	1,708,179	3.42%	9.45%
10.0 to 20.0 million	13,891,152	399,731	1,889,749	2.88%	13.60%
20.0 million or more	38,700,754	1,015,036	9,094,209	2.62%	23.50%

Source: Internal Revenue Service, Statistics of Income Division, September 2010, *Estate Tax Returns Filed in 2009, by Tax Status and Size of Gross Estate.*

[a] In 2009, most tax returns were filed for deaths occurring in 2008, for which the estate tax exemption level was $2 million. However, due to filing extensions, a limited number of returns were filed in 2009 for deaths occurring prior to 2008, when the filing threshold may have been below $2 million.

[b] IRS notes that this estimate for farm assets should be used with caution due to the small sample of returns on which it is based.

[c] As reported in *Estate Tax Returns Filed in 2009*, data for the "under 2.0 million" and "2.0 to 3.5 million" estate value classes on two categories of business estate assets, real estate partnerships and other non-corporate business assets, were combined to prevent disclosure of individual taxpayer information. In Table 4, the combined value class totals for these two respective asset categories are disaggregated by using the ratio of gross estate value for the "2.0 to 3.5 million" value class to the gross estate value for the "under 2.0 million" value class, 22.0.

Though farm and business decedents may have other taxable assets—such as equities and cash—the burden on farm and business assets alone is quite small relative to other assets. Thus, removing the estate and gift tax or lowering the rates in general will have a much greater effect on non-farm and non-business assets.

Table 4 presents detailed data on farm and business assets by gross estate value. Relatively large farm estates, those valued between $2 million and $3.5 million, comprise a relatively larger share of total estate value for that estate size category. Overall, however, farm estates appear to be evenly distributed across the estate size categories. Note that farm assets account for approximately 3.25% of total taxable estate value.

In contrast to farm estates, assets typically associated with non-farm businesses are concentrated in estates valued over $10 million. In fact, of the $14.1 billion in total business assets in estates, over $11.0 billion (77.7%) is held in those estates valued over $10 million. As a consequence, smaller-business taxable estates, those valued at less than $10 million, contribute very little to the estate and gift tax base.

In summary, repeal of the estate and gift tax would clearly achieve the policy objective of relief for estates composed of farm and small-business assets. Farm assets and business assets, however, represent a relatively small share of total taxable estate value, approximately 17.1% at the most.

End Notes

[1] A full discussion of the estate tax as a tax on capital and saving can be found in the following: Gale, William G., James R. Hines Jr., and Joel Slemrod, eds., *Rethinking Estate and Gift Taxation*, The Brookings Institution, 2001.

[2] The value of the stock would be "stepped-up" to the value at the time of death. The inheritor could liquidate the stock immediately and avoid taxation completely.

[3] There are special provisions for payment of estate taxes on family businesses given the liquidity constraints specific to these types of estates.

[4] Joint Committee on Taxation, "Estimated Budget Effects of the 'Tax Relief, Unemployment Insurance Reauthorization, and Job Creation Act of 2010,'" JCX-54-10, December 10, 2010. available.

[5] Elizabeth McNichol, "State Taxes on Inherited Wealth Remain Common: 22 States Levy an Estate or Inheritance Tax," *Center on Budget and Policy Priorities*, April 10, 2009.

[6] Internal Revenue Service, Statistics of Income Division, October 2009, *Estate Tax Returns Filed in 2008, by Tax Status and Size of Gross Estate*, available at http://www.irs.gov/taxstats/indtaxstats/article/0,,id=210646,00.html.

[7] The latest available estate tax data are for the 2008 tax year. Total number of non-infant deaths in 2008, as reported in "Births, Marriages, Divorces, and Deaths: Provisional Data for 2008," *National Vital Statistics Reports, vol. 57, no. 19*, July 29, 2009, was 2,425,400. The data is available at http://www.cdc.gov/nchs/data/nvsr/nvsr57/nvsr57_19.pdf.

[8] For a detailed history of the estate and gift tax as well as an explanation of current law, see CRS Report 95-416, *Federal Estate, Gift, and Generation-Skipping Taxes: A Description of Current Law*, by John R. Luckey.

In: Estate and Gift Taxes
Editor: Jacob A. Hughes
ISBN: 978-1-62100-516-2

Chapter 6

ESTATE TAXES AND FAMILY BUSINESSES: ECONOMIC ISSUES*

Jane G. Gravelle and Steven Maguire

SUMMARY

The 2001 tax revision began a phaseout of the estate tax, by increasing exemptions and lowering rates. The estate tax is scheduled to be repealed in 2010 and a provision to tax appreciation on inherited assets (in excess of a limit) will be substituted. The 2001 tax provisions sunset, however, so that absent a change making them permanent the estate tax will revert, in 2011, to prior, pre-2001 law. Proposals to make the repeal permanent, or to significantly increase the exemptions and lower the rate, are under consideration.

Discussions of the estate tax have focused particularly on the effects on family businesses, including farms, and the perception that the estate tax unfairly burdens family businesses because much of the estate value is held in illiquid assets (e.g., land, buildings, and equipment). The estate tax may even force the liquidation of family businesses. A special family business deduction, the Qualified Family Owned Business Interest Exemption (QFOBI) was enacted in 1997. Because of higher exemptions and a previous cap on the combined regular and small business exemption, this provision is no longer relevant. If, however, the estate tax repeal sunsets, QFOBI will again be germane.

---

* This is an edited, reformatted and augmented version of a Congressional Research Service publication, CRS Report for Congress RL33070, from www.crs.gov, dated January 6, 2010.

On December 3, 2009, the House passed H.R. 4154, the Permanent Estate Tax Relief for Families, Farmers, and Small Businesses Act of 2009. H.R. 4154 makes the 2009 provisions, which allow a $3.5 million exemption and a 45% tax rate, permanent. In the Senate, leaders have indicated that they will consider estate tax legislation in 2010. Proposals considered in the Senate during the 111th Congress have included the extension of the 2009 estate tax provisions to 2010, permanently repealing the tax, and increasing the exemption and/or decreasing the rate. At the same time, some proposals focused on allowing an expanded business exemption.

Despite this attention to family business, evidence suggests that only a small fraction of estates with small or family business interests have paid the estate tax (about 3.5% for businesses in general, and 5% for farmers, compared to 2% for all estates). Recent estimates suggest that only a tiny fraction of family-owned businesses (less than 1/2 of 1%) are subject to the estate tax but do not have readily available resources to pay the tax. Thus, while the estate tax may be a burden on those families, the problem is confined to a small group.

If the estate tax is repealed, QFOBI will allow an exemption for some or all of business assets in about one-third to one-half of estates with more than half of their assets in these businesses, but the value of the exemption will be reduced because the general exemption has increased. If the estate tax repeal is made permanent, liquidity will cease being a problem, although family businesses may be more likely than other estates to be affected by the capital gains provisions. Exposure to the estate tax, if it is reinstated, would be significantly decreased by increases in either the family business or general exemptions. The report also discusses an uncapped exemption and an uncapped exemption targeted at liquidity issues.

INTRODUCTION

The Economic Growth and Tax Relief Reconciliation Act of 2001 (EGTRRA) phased out the estate tax by gradually increasing the exemption and lowering the rate; the tax will be eliminated in 2010. A provision providing for carryover basis for assets transferred at death will replace the current step-up in basis. This latter provision would require heirs, when selling inherited assets, to pay tax on the gain that existed at the time of death, in addition to any appreciation since transfer. (A $1.3 million exemption would be allowed, with an additional $3 million for a surviving spouse.) The repeal of the estate tax and the provision for carryover basis is sunsetted and, absent legislative change, will revert to pre-2001 law in 2011, with an exemption of

$1 million and a top statutory tax rate of 55%. The law will also revert to the prior rule of a stepped-up basis for assets, where no capital gains tax would be paid on appreciation of assets existing at the time of death.

Proposals to make the repeal permanent, to significantly increase the exemptions and lower the rate, or to make current law permanent are under consideration. On December 3, 2009, the House passed H.R. 4154, the Permanent Estate Tax Relief for Families, Farmers, and Small Businesses Act of 2009. H.R. 4154 makes the 2009 provisions, which allow a $3.5 million exemption and a 45% tax rate, permanent. In the Senate, leaders have indicated that they will consider estate tax legislation in 2010. Proposals considered in the Senate during the 111th Congress have included the extension of the 2009 estate tax provisions to 2010, permanently repealing the tax, and increasing the exemption and/or decreasing the rate. At the same time, some proposals focused on allowing an expanded business exemption.

Discussions about the estate tax have focused particular attention on the effects on family businesses, including farms.[1] Many policy makers and observers have maintained that the estate tax unfairly burdens family businesses because much of the estate value is held in illiquid assets (e.g., land, buildings, and equipment). [2] The estate tax, it is suggested, forces these businesses to liquidate vital assets to pay the tax. Critics of the estate tax posit that, in some cases, liquidating the business completely may be the only option.

Prior law contained a special deduction for family-owned businesses (the qualified family-owned business interest deduction, or QFOBI) to address this issue; this deduction was capped so that the total of the normal exemption and the family business exemption could not exceed $1.3 million. The deduction was also contingent on meeting a number of qualifying rules. QFOBI is currently irrelevant since the exemption is $1.5 million (and was repealed by EGTRRA for 2004 and beyond), but will play a role again if the EGTRRA provisions sunset. The estate tax (both under current and permanent rules) contains some other provisions that may make the payment of the tax easier for family-owned businesses. Qualifying estates can pay the tax in installments over a maximum of 10 years after a five-year deferral, and can value their land as currently used rather than at fair market value.[3] Family-owned business may also be more likely to benefit from minority and marketability discounts, which allow a lower valuation if the property is held by several heirs with a minority interest or is otherwise difficult to sell.[4]

This report discusses the general issue of family-owned businesses, and then discusses the consequences of several options including making no revisions (and hence returning to pre-2001 law in 2011); making the repeal of the estate tax permanent; and, modifying exemptions while retaining an estate tax. This latter discussion considers expanding or altering the existing general or business exemptions, providing an exemption for all business assets (no dollar ceiling or other restrictions), or modifying the QFOBI-type exemption to eliminate a cliff effect that currently exists because only estates with half of the assets in a business were eligible for the special deduction.

FAMILY BUSINESS ASSETS IN THE ESTATE TAX BASE

Although much attention has been devoted to the effect of the estate tax on family farms and businesses, and in particular the forced liquidation of family businesses and business assets, very few family businesses pay the estate tax and very little of the estate tax is collected from family businesses (and none from truly small businesses due to the exemption levels). Of those estates with family business assets, most would appear to be able to pay the tax, as discussed below.

Farm and business assets appear to account for around 11%-12% of taxable estate assets, and perhaps a little more because these data are from 2003 when some QFOBI still existed.[5]

Some data reported in another CRS report[6] are instructive regarding the ability of family-owned businesses to pay the tax. Of taxable estates in 2006, 6.3% reported farm assets and 43.2% reported business assets. However, while around 50.0% of taxable estate tax returns report some business or farm assets (there is some overlap between the farm and business numbers), only 1.4 % of estates were those where farm assets were at least half of the estate and only 1.6% of estates had business assets that accounted for half of the estate. Farm assets in these returns accounted for 0.6% of estate value and business assets 4.1%. Since estates with less than half of their assets in farm or business assets would have other sources (from the estate itself) to pay the tax, only this small fraction of estates would presumably have to deal with possible liquidation, and these estates were targeted by QFOBI. Table 1 and Table 2 below report the percentage of estates with business assets by estate size and the value of the business assets as a percentage of the estate by estate size for returns filed in 2006, respectively.

This same report also estimated that only 3.3% of business owners face the estate tax, and about 5% of farmers do. This share is slightly larger than the share of all decedents, where less than 2% pay the tax, reflecting the higher average wealth of the farm and business owners.

Table 1. Percentage of Estates with Business Assets by Type of Asset and Estate Size in 2006

Size of Gross Estate	Number	Real Estate Partnerships	Closely Held Stock	Farm Assets	Limited Partnerships	Other Non-corp. Bus. Assets
All Returns	49,050	6.9%	15.4%	7.3%	15.7%	11.2%
1 to 2.5 million	16,865	3.7%	9.5%	7.4%	9.72%	5.7%
2.5 to 5.0 million	24,486	6.8%	15.1%	6.8%	15.1%	11.8%
5.0 to 10.0 million	5,953	11.0%	24.2%	7.8%	26.4%	16.7%
10.0 to 20 million	1,708	18.7%	35.2%	9.1%	34.2%	24.2%
over 20.0 million	939	26.7%	48.3%	10.5%	46.4%	37.8%
Taxable Returns	22,798	5.8%	12.3%	6.3%	15.9%	9.1%
1 to 2.5 million	6,523	3.1%	6.4%	6.1%	11.5%	3.3%
2.5 to 5.0 million	11,994	5.2%	10.6%	5.9%	13.9%	8.9%
5.0 to 10.0 million	2,664	7.3%	19.6%	7.0%	23.2%	14.0%
10.0 to 20 million	1,004	16.1%	30.1%	8.7%	31.9%	19.5%
over 20.0 million	614	2.5%	44.5%	10.4%	45.9%	36.0%

Source: Internal Revenue Service, Statistics of Income, *Estate Tax Returns Filed in 2006.*

If one considers the ability to pay the tax out of all non-business assets, then if half of the estate is held in other assets, given a tax rate of 55%, and since assets are excluded from the estate through general exemptions as well, the non-business assets would generally be adequate to pay the tax (since the tax as a share of the estate will usually be below 50% of the value). According to the data reported above, about 20% of returns with farm assets (1.4/6.4) have more than 50% of assets in farm assets, suggesting that less than 1% of decedents with farm assets would not have enough non-business resources to pay the tax. For business owners, only about 4% involve returns where business assets are more than one-half of the estate. Thus, by this calculation, less than 1/10 of 1% of business owners would not have enough non-business resources to pay the tax.

Evidence suggests that most of these estates could still pay the estate tax out of liquid assets alone (cash, bonds, and publicly traded stock) under pre-2001 law, and thus would not have to cash in any other property (such as a home or other real estate). A recent study by the Congressional Budget Office[7] (hereafter the CBO study), examined data from 2000 to determine the fraction of estates that would not have enough liquid assets (stocks, bonds, cash, etc) to pay the tax. (They also indicated that liquid assets would be somewhat higher because it was not able to include assets held in trusts in this study.) For farms, it found that, in 2000, 8% of farm estates could not pay the tax out of liquid assets. Given that an estimated 5% of farm estates pay the tax, less than one-half of one percent of farm decedents would be faced with selling any non-liquid assets (whether business or other) to pay the estate tax.

The CBO study did not examine business owners broadly, since it restricted its examination to those business returns that were eligible for QFOBI, and which, therefore, by definition, have estates where business assets account for over half of the estate. These estates are thus much less likely than the average business owner to have sufficient liquid assets to pay the estate tax. But even among these estates, only 32% did not have sufficient liquid assets to pay the estate tax. Thus, it seems likely that the shares of businesses overall that could not pay the tax out of liquid assets are similar in magnitude, and probably smaller, than farms.

These estimates suggest that only a tiny fraction of family-owned businesses (less than 1/2 of 1%) do not have enough readily available resources to pay the estate tax. Thus, while the estate tax may be a burden on those families, the problem is confined to a small group. In addition, businesses that do not have other assets sufficient to pay the tax still have the option of paying in installments, borrowing, or selling a partial interest in the business. On average these businesses also received significant minority discounts, so that the estate tax owed would be smaller relative to the value of the property.[8]

Table 2. Percentage of Estate Value Held in Business Assets by Type of Asset and Estate Size in 2003

Size of Gross Estate	Amount (Thousands of Dollars)	Real Estate Partnerships	Closely Held Stock	Farm Assets	Limited Partnerships	Other Non-corp. Bus. Assets
All Returns	211,460,077	1.9%	6.4%	0.8%	1.99%	1.5%
1 to 2.5 million	27,942,870	0.7%	1.9%	1.0%	0.52%	0.6%
2.5 to 5.0 million	71,955,444	1.2%	3.1%	0.8%	1.37%	0.9%
5.0 to 10.0 million	34,142,415	1.8%	5.1%	0.8%	2.28%	1.0%
10.0 to 20 million	22,983,958	3.0%	6.9%	0.8%	2.66%	1.6%
over 20.0 million	54,430,509	2.9%	13.9%	0.7%	4.68%	3.1%
Taxable Returns	116098783	1.30%	4.84%	0.7%	2.9%	1.47%
1 to 2.5 million	11,087,676	0.56%	1.37%	0.6%	1.0%	0.3%
2.5 to 5.0 million	35,749,137	0.67%	2.71%	0.6%	1.2%	0.6%
5.0 to 10.0 million	18,224,809	0.72%	3.79%	0.8%	2.1%	0.7%
10.0 to 20 million	13,562,562	1.79%	6.51%	0.6%	3.9%	1.0%
over 20.0 million	37,470,301	2.57%	9.77%	0.7%	5.2%	3.0%

Source: Internal Revenue Service, Statistics of Income, *Estate Tax Returns Filed in 2006*.

POLICY OPTIONS FOR ADDRESSING FAMILY BUSINESS ISSUES

There are several alternative policy options for addressing family business estate tax issues. If EGTRRA sunsets, the QFOBI deduction will once again become relevant: the first section below discusses general issues surrounding this provision. The following section discusses the implications for family businesses of making the estate tax repeal permanent. The remaining sections address various revisions within the framework of retaining an estate tax, including an increase in either the QFOBI or general exemption, an unlimited business assets deduction, and an alternative business deduction that would target illiquidity but address a problem with QFOBI due to a "cliff" effect.

Permanent Effects of the Current Law (No Legislative Change and a Reversion to Pre-2001 Law in 2011)

If no legislative action is taken, the estate tax exemption will rise through 2009 (to $3.5 million) and the rate will fall to 45%. In 2010, the estate tax will be repealed, but in 2011 the rules will revert to those that existed before EGTRRA. Under these rules, which were last revised in 1997, the general estate tax exemption will be $1 million, the tax rate will be 55%,[9] and a QFOBI exemption will be allowed, but the combined exemption will still be limited to $1.3 million. Thus, the effective QFOBI exemption is capped at $300,000.

Returning to the status quo and QFOBI raises several issues, a key one being that the real value of the cap has fallen compared to pre-2001 law, so more qualifying estates will be subject to tax. Thus, it might be appropriate to increase the overall cap.

The QFOBI provisions are subject to a number of restrictions designed to ensure that the business is family owned (the decedent and decedent's family must own 50% of the business, or own 30% of a business that is 70% owned by two families, or 90% owned by three families). The business cannot have been publicly traded in the last three years, no more than 35% of the business income may be personal holding company income, and the business must have been owned and operated for five of the past eight years. Heirs are required to continue the business for the next 10 years to avoid recapture. Finally, QFOBI applies only to estates where at least 50% of the assets are family business assets. There are also restrictions on the amount of working capital which are designed to prevent the movement of cash and other liquid assets into the business to increase the deduction or allow an estate to qualify.

The rules designed to target the QFOBI provisions have been criticized due to their complexity. For example, Michael Graetz and Ian Shapiro write:

> Everyone now agrees—regardless of which side of the issue they are on—that QFOBI has been a complete and utter failure... It did not solve anything. QFOBI has so many requirements, so many structures and pitfalls, that very few family businesses have obtained any tax relief at all because of it.[10]

This is a harsh criticism, and it is not necessarily supported by the data. According to the CBO study, for 2000, about 1% of taxable returns claimed the QFOBI and about 1.4% of estates filing returns did so. Given the evidence that only about 3% of taxable estates had more than half of assets in business (and recognizing that some of these estates become nontaxable because of QFOBI), it appears that about one-third to one-half of these businesses qualified for QFOBI. QFOBI's scope was limited primarily because it was allowed only for those estates where a majority of assets were in the business. Other estates with more than half of their assets in business assets might not have qualified because the business assets were not fully a family business (i.e., largely owned by no more than three families), or because the heirs chose to sell the business.

The QFOBI provision does, nevertheless, raise questions of equity and can produce some economic distortions, as well as complications.

The special business deduction does create some issues of equity—as is the case with any type of special tax exemption. Those with eligible business assets will pay lower taxes on the same amount of wealth than those without such assets. This inequity is a necessary price of targeting a specific group, and must be weighed against the benefits of the QFOBI targeted tax benefit generating a smaller revenue loss than a broader exemption.

QFOBI also creates economic distortions. It induces taxpayers to shift assets into business form, or, alternatively, to avoid liquidating a business when that outcome would be most desirable. How these incentives work depends, in part, on the kind of exemption. Consider an unlimited exemption for business assets. For taxable estates and a 55% estate tax rate, a dollar shifted from non-business assets to business assets saves 55 cents. Or, from another perspective, if business assets earned the same return as other assets, one would be willing to pay $2.22 ($1/(1-0.55)) for a business asset that normally sells for a dollar. Or if asset prices are fixed, one would be willing to accept a rate of return that was as much as 55% smaller in a business investment than in other investments.

The QFOBI provision was limited to estates with 50% or more of gross estate value in business assets, and was capped. Thus, very large estates that had already used up the cap would have no incentive to shift assets, as would estates with so few business assets they would be unlikely to qualify. However smaller estates that fell below the cap and were eligible would have the same incentives as described above for the unlimited simple exemptions (each dollar shifted would, with a 55% tax rate, save 55 cents). And estates that were very close to eligibility would have powerful incentives to shift business investments, though a "cliff" effect. To use a simple example, from pre-2001 law (a $675,000 regular exemption and a maximum of $1.3 million with the business deduction, but using a flat rate for illustrative purposes), if business assets were 45% and the estate totaled $3 million, by shifting $150,000 in assets from non-business to business would save $343,750 (0.55 times $625,000). Even if the assets were virtually worthless, as long as they were not shifted for a long time (causing forgone earnings), one would be better off making the investment. Cliffs are generally to be avoided in devising minimally distorting tax rules.

A third response to this cliff effect would be to overvalue business assets; these rules also magnify existing incentives to undervalue other assets. This response does not distort investment but it does use up resources in estate planning and causes unintended benefits and revenue losses. The cliff effect can also intensify the existing incentives to remove non-business assets from the estate. All of the special business deduction provisions create incentives to recharacterize as much of the estate as possible as business assets.

The provision of QFOBI that required keeping the business in the family after the decedent's death (that recaptured all or part of the tax when the business was ended) also produces economic distortions. The provision affects the allocation of capital and the employment of the heirs. This rule, of course, was intended to target those family businesses whose failure to continue was due to the estate tax.

Finally, the QFOBI provisions complicate administration and compliance. For example, there are rules to prevent holding of cash and other liquid assets in the business; since all businesses must have some cash or near-cash assets available, it is necessary to determine what level of working capital is needed in the business. Such a provision would be necessary with any form of business exemption, since without such rules non-business assets could be lodged in the business. There are also provisions to deal with ownership and control by the family, and whether someone has materially participated in the business.

From this analysis, it seems clear that QFOBI went a long way towards achieving its objective, but it does reflect problems that arose as a result of the targeting of the provision. These problems do not mean that QFOBI was not desirable, as it reflects a specific trade-off of the benefits of addressing the liquidity problem at a minimal revenue cost against the efficiency, equity, and administrative costs. The difficulties in qualifying for QFOBI were perhaps largely because the provision was targeted at family-owned businesses that dominated the estate, not estates that were less clearly "family-owned."

Effect of Making Estate Tax Repeal Permanent

If the estate tax repeal is made permanent, the liquidity issue will disappear for years 2010 and after. However, given that less than 3% of estates could encounter a liquidity problem (returns with more than half of assets in the business, 1.4% for farms and 1.6% for other businesses), this repeal would be very costly from the federal budget perspective if the only objective were to deal with the family-owned business issue.

There is no liquidity problem with this tax regime, because there would be no estate tax and the capital gains tax would apply only if the assets are sold.

This new regime would, however, raise some different issues regarding the effects on the family business. Theoretically, under an income tax, "all accretions to wealth" over a given period of time should be taxed. Traditionally the U.S. income tax has not imposed a tax on gain until realized, and has allowed stepped up basis for appreciated assets so that no tax on the gain accumulated by the decedent is taxed on sale by the heirs. The estate tax provided a backstop to this exemption so that large accumulations of gain would be taxed under the estate tax. The Economic Growth and Tax Relief Reconciliation Act of 2001 (EGTRRA) addressed this issue through changing the asset valuation to a "carry-over" basis regime when the estate tax is repealed in 2010. Under carry-over basis, the heir assumes the basis of the decedent. In other words, the heir "steps into the shoes" of the decedent and would pay capital gains taxes (upon sale of the asset) based on the appreciation from the original purchase price (or value).[11] Congress included in EGTRRA a $3 million spousal exclusion and a $1.3 million general exclusion for capital gains on transferred assets to reduce the tax burden on heirs who sell inherited assets.

Family businesses, and small businesses more generally, likely have significant unrealized capital gains when the proprietor dies. One study estimated the amount of unrealized capital gains held at death for estates valued under $5 million to be approximately 35% of the estates' value (approximately $34 billion in the aggregate in 1998).[12] Any business with total assets valued less than the exemption amount, which is $1.5 million in 2005 rising to $3.5 million in 2009, would not pay any federal estate taxes.[13] In addition, the value of all assets in the business would be stepped up to the value at the time of death. Based on the above estimate of the portion of estate value represented by untaxed capital gains, the step-up treatment confers a significant tax benefit to these estates. The estate tax regime with the stepped-up basis on transferred assets clearly favors these relatively small business estates, sheltering a total of approximately $34 billion in capital gains from taxation. Some have noted that farms in particular benefit from this treatment because, among other reasons, "the income tax basis of raised animals, for farmers on the cash method of accounting, is zero."[14]

When the estate tax is repealed in 2010, the stepped-up basis is replaced with carry-over basis treatment (explained earlier). Congress, however, included a safe harbor for $1.3 million in capital gains passed to a non-spouse. Using the 35% unrealized capital gains estimate above, this treatment would, on average, shelter an estate valued at approximately $3.7 million from capital gains tax liability (if heirs sold bequeathed assets).[15] The smaller the portion of unrealized capital gains, the larger the overall estate size that could avoid capital gains taxation. The difficulty in assessing and confirming the decedent's basis would create an incentive to overstate basis to avoid capital gains taxes.

Theory suggests that the potential capital gains tax liability for the very large estates may generate dynastic asset hoarding. For the largest estates in the NBER study cited above—those with assets over $10 million—the unrealized capital gains comprised over 56% of the estate's total value. The unrealized gains are predominantly business assets in these very large estates; 72.3% of the unrealized gain is held in active farm or business assets. Over time, the potential tax liability would likely increase along with unrealized capital gains further reducing the probability of capital gain realization.

For family businesses that heirs wish to continue, the potential tax liability and asset liquidity are not primary concerns under the carry-over basis regime. In contrast, for heirs who wish to liquidate the business, in particular business with significant untaxed capital gains, the carry-over basis treatment may generate significant tax implications. The disincentive would contribute to a “lock-in” effect, likely growing with each generation.

Increasing the QFOBI Dollar Limits

With no legislative changes, the effective QFOBI exemption has fallen, due to the increase in the general estate tax exemption. The QFOBI dollar limit could be increased, which would reduce the number of firms that are taxable The CBO study provides some estimates of the effects of a general exemption that can also be used to infer some of the effects of raising the combined QFOBI and general exemption. In 2000, 485 estates claiming QFOBI paid tax, and 164 of those had insufficient liquidity to pay the tax. With a $1 million general exemption, a rise to a $1.5 million total (allowing a $500,000 QFOBI deduction) would reduce those numbers by about 50%—to 223 and 82 respectively. Allowing a $2 million total limit (a $1 million QFOBI) would reduce the numbers by about around two thirds—to 135 and 62 respectively.

Retaining the Estate Tax and Expanding the General Exemption and/or Lowering Rates

Another option is to retain the estate tax and stepped-up basis, but increase the general exemption, lower the rates, or both. This approach is much more costly than increasing the QFOBI exemption since it would apply to all estates. But it would alter the taxation of both business and non-business estates substantially. In 2000, 52,000 estates owed taxes and 2,834 (5.5%) had insufficient liquid assets to pay the tax. At that time the general estate tax exemption was $675,000. Increasing the exemption to $1.5 million (the 2005 value), $2 million (the 2006- 2008 level), and $3.5 million (the 2009 level) would reduce the number of taxable estates by 70%, 88% and 93% respectively. For all levels of exemptions, between 5 and 6% of taxable estates would not have enough liquid assets to pay the tax. These results suggest that most estates are in the lower part of the asset value distribution, and that large estates have significant liquid assets. In the case of farmers, the proportional reduction would be greater: 82%, 92%, and 96% respectively. The share (although not the number) of estates that would have insufficient liquidity to pay the tax would rise from 8% to 9%, 12%, and 20% respectively. These values suggest that the share of liquid assets in farm estates becomes smaller as estates become larger.

In a different study, the Tax Policy Center found that in 2011, with a $1 million exemption, there would be 760 taxable estates with farm or businesses comprising more than 50% of assets; with a $2 million exemption there would be only 210, and with a $3.5 million exemption only 50.[16] These reductions in the tax burden on business assets are, however, accompanied by even more important general reductions in estate taxes, so that, if the objective is to provide relief for family businesses, it is not target efficient.

Clearly an increase in the general exemption would dramatically reduce the number of taxable estates with family-owned businesses.

A General Exemption for Business Property

An alternative approach to raising the general exemption would be to provide an exemption for all business property. With all business property deducted, no estate would have taxes that required the liquidation of the business. With a tax rate of around 50%, about one-quarter of the estate would be used to pay taxes if business assets were 50% of the total. Since farm and business assets are slightly over 10% of assets in taxable estates, the cost of this provision would be slightly over 10% of the cost of repealing the estate tax altogether.

An open-ended business exemption would eliminate the cliff effects of the current QFOBI, since all estates with any business property would be eligible to exclude business assets. But, it would also increase the number of estates that would claim a special deduction and increase the amount of assets that receive special tax treatment. The increase in the number of estates and the amount of assets receiving favorable tax treatment would also create distorting effects, encouraging disproportionate investment in business assets across a broad range of estates.

An open ended deduction would also be much more costly than the current QFOBI deductions and would much less precisely target family-owned businesses. Recall that about 40% of taxable estates have business or farm assets, but only about 3% have more than half of their assets in business assets, and only about 1% qualify for QFOBI. In addition to expanding the scope of coverage, estates would receive a much larger deduction with an unlimited business exemption.

A general business exemption could still have a dollar cap, which would reduce the cost, relative to an open-ended deduction. Any type of deduction aimed at certain assets would still require rules to prevent abuse (such as limits on cash transferred into the business) and would still create inequities and incentives, although there would no longer be incentives to overvalue business assets or undervalue other assets to qualify for the deduction, as in the case of the cliff in QFOBI.

AN EXEMPTION FOR BUSINESS PROPERTY TARGETED TO LIQUIDITY

Another option is to target the liquidity issue specifically by establishing a business exemption based on the availability of non-business assets to pay the tax. In this case, the business exemption would be a function of both the size of the estate and the share of the estate that is held in business assets. This targeted approach might provide significant revenue savings relative to an exemption that simply excludes all business assets. This approach is illustrated using a simplified example with a flat rate estate tax rate. (Recall that the federal estate tax before the EGTRRA 2001 changes included graduated rates, and the exemption was actually a credit for the taxes that would have been due on the amount up to the exemption amount. The graduated rates (if retained in a final law), however, would need to be taken into consideration under the option described here.)

Congress might wish to consider the policy option of limiting the business exemption so that the tax is no more than the liquidated value of the non-business assets. The reasoning behind this policy objective is readily apparent. Optimally, the estate tax should not force a family business (or farm) to liquidate business assets that generate income, particularly if the business is to continue in the family after the original owner dies. In this scenario, the tax on the entire estate should match the value (at most) of non-business assets.

For example, consider an estate where the total value of all assets in the estate is $10 million, the regular exemption is $1 million, and assume the tax rate is a flat 55% (a simplified version of the pre-2001 tax law rules). Further assume that three-quarters (75%) of the value is held in business assets. If all business assets were exempted, there would be an exemption of $8.5 million ($7.5 million for the business assets and an additional $1 million regular exemption) and the tax due would be $825,000. Suppose instead that an exemption is set precisely so that the tax equals the liquidated value of the all non-business assets (or \$2.5 million). This outcome requires a total exemption of \$5,454,545 (\$2.5 million divided by the tax rate of 55% plus the \$1 million regular exemption). Or, stated differently, the tax on what is left in the estate after the business exemption and the regular exemption amount must generate \$2.5 million in taxes at the 55% rate.

The estate tax is 55% times (\$10,000,000—\$1,000,000—\$4,454,545), or \$2.5 million, which is exactly the value of non-business assets. In this case, the effective tax rate is 25% (\$2.5 million divided by \$10 million). No business faces a liquidity problem, there is no cliff, and the revenue cost of the exemption is less than what would be the case if all business assets were exempt from the estate tax.

In contrast, if exemptions are allowed for all estates, the revenue loss is larger than necessary to target the liquidity issue. If estates are excluded based on a fixed share of business assets (a "cliff" at 50% of total asset value in business assets for example), as in the QFOBI, the rules create very powerful incentives to shift assets to business uses to meet the qualification threshold. This effect will become more powerful if the exemption is unlimited. If the rules precisely target the business assets to deal with the liquidity issue, as described in the previous example, there is also an incentive to shift assets into business uses. In the example provided above, there is an implicit 100% tax on non-business assets, which also creates a powerful incentive to shift assets into the business—not as powerful as a cliff effect, but more powerful than a simple exemption.

For that reason policy makers could opt to modify the formula such that the tax does not consume the entire value of the non-business assets. For example, if every dollar shifted into a business asset increased tax liability by less than a dollar, the incentive effect to reclassify assets is muted. The equation below allows a variety of changes in taxable portion of non-business assets.[17] The variable "*d*" is the portion of the non-business assets that would be used to pay the tax. Reducing *d*, reduces the estate tax burden on non-business assets. If policy makers chose to only devote 60% of non-business assets (and 0% of the business assets) to pay the tax, then *d*=0.60.[18]

$$E^b = A^t - E^s - \frac{A^{nb} d}{t}$$

where,

t is the estate tax rate;
A^t is the total value of all assets in the estate;
A^{nb} is the total value of non-business/farm assets;
A^b is the total value of business/farm assets in the estate;
E^s is standard estate tax exemption amount; and
E^b is the business/farm asset exemption.

Table 3 illustrates the revenue loss associated with these alternatives for three $10 million estates, assuming a 55% flat rate, and a $1 million general exemption. Note that the difference between the 55% tax and the unlimited business exemption is that the business exemption includes the general exemption when it is smaller, rather than being added to the business exemptions (i.e., each differs by $550,000 which is 55% of $1 million). This adjustment could be made to a general unlimited exemption and would reduce the revenue cost significantly.

Table 3. Revenue Cost of Options for a $10 Million Estate with a 55% Flat Tax Rate (revenue cost in $ millions)

Share of Non-business Assets Paid in Tax, the *D* Parameter	Share of Estate in Business Assets in Three Estates		
	Estate I	Estate II	Estate III
	75%	50%	25%
1.00	2.000	0.000	0.000
0.90	2.250	0.500	0.000
0.80	2.500	0.950	0.000
0.70	2.750	1.450	0.000
0.60	3.000	1.950	0.450
0.55	3.125	2.200	0.825
Unlimited Exemption	3.675	2.750	1.375

Source: Calculations based on equations in the text.

Notes: The tax rate is 55%; the estate value is $10 million, the value of the standard exemption is $1 million; share of business assets is set at 25%, 50%, and 75%) and *d* ranges from 0.55 to 1.

Adjusting the exemption of business size in this fashion allows revenue savings for the federal government relative to an unlimited exemption, and eliminates the cliff effect. And, although the equations seem complex, this system would simplify estate planning because qualifying for the exemption would not be as important. Shifting one dollar from non-business to business use would save the taxpayer less than one dollar, with the size depending on the share parameter (i.e., if the *d* parameter is set at 70%, each dollar shifted saves 70 cents, more than with an unlimited exemption, where it saves 55 cents).

Figure 1 exhibits the effective tax rate on a hypothetical estate depending on the business share of assets. If the entire estate is business assets (on the left side of the graph), there is no tax. Each line represents a different value for the policy parameter *d*. Recall that the closer *d* gets to one, the greater the estate tax burden.

This type of sliding scale means that the fraction of business assets deducted varies depending on the concentration of business assets in the estate. This outcome may be perceived as unfair; at the same time, the average inequity between those with significant business assets and those with no business assets or only a small share would be reduced.

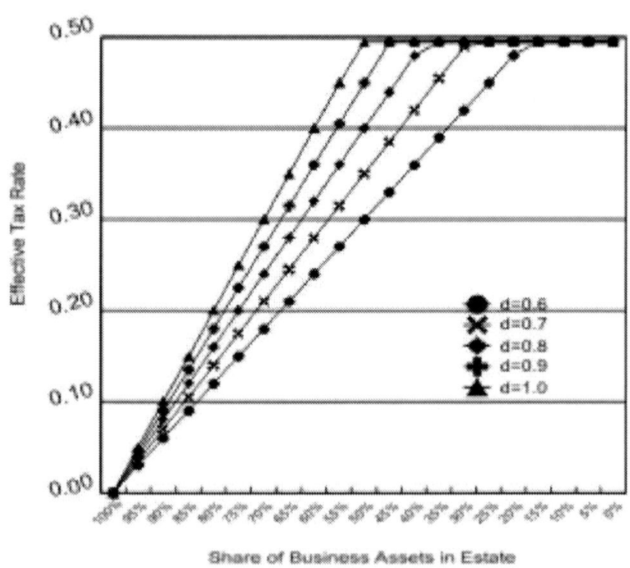

Note: d=share of non-business assets paid in estate tax.

Figure 1. Hypothetical Estate Tax Burden by Share of Business Assets Under Five Policy Parameters.

CONCLUSION

Although the evidence suggests that only a small portion of businesses and farms are subject to the estate tax, there may still be a concern about the impact on those particular businesses.

The options discussed for addressing family-owned business issues involve trade-offs between the revenue cost of providing exemptions to a broader group than necessary to address the issue (including repealing the estate tax in general) and other issues. The more targeted the proposal, the more administrative, distorting, and equity issues arise, but the smaller the revenue cost.

The QFOBI deduction, which is the most targeted of the options considered in this paper, created a particularly difficult problem due to its cliff effect, and the final approach discussed is aimed at eliminating the cliff effect and providing a sliding scale deduction targeted at liquidity issues. Of course, if policy makers desire to eliminate the estate tax as provided in 2010, and there are arguments for doing so, the liquidity issue would disappear. But the revenue effect would be significant and the substitute capital gains provisions would exacerbate lock-in effects.

APPENDIX. CALCULATION OF THE BUSINESS EXEMPTION

Algebraically, the equations are the following:

$$t(A^t - E^s - E^b) = A^{nb} \qquad (1)$$

$$A^t = A^b + A^{nb} \qquad (2)$$

where,

t is the estate tax rate;
A^t is the total value of all assets in the estate;
A^{nb} is the total value of non-business/farm assets;
A^b is the total value of business/farm assets in the estate;
E^s is standard estate tax exemption amount; and
E^b is the business/farm asset exemption.

The next step in determining the appropriate value of the business exemption, E^b, is to rearrange equation (1). The following equation, (1)*, for determining the appropriate business exemption if the policy objective is to match the estate tax due to the entire liquidated value of non-business assets.

$$E^b = A^t - E^s - \frac{A^{nb}}{t} \qquad (1)^*$$

Equation (3) below allows a variety of changes in taxable portion of non-business assets. The variable "*d* " is the portion of the non-business assets that would be used to pay the tax. In equation (1)*, $d = 1$, or the total value of non-business assets are used to pay the tax. Reducing *d*, reduces the estate tax burden on non-business assets. For example, if policy makers chose to only devote 60% of non-business assets (and 0% of the business assets) to pay the tax, then $d = 0.60$.[19]

$$E^b = A^t - E^s - \frac{A^{nb} d}{t} \qquad (3)$$

End Notes

[1] For a discussion of the political issues surrounding the estate tax issue, including the issue of family businesses, see Michael J. Graetz and Ian Shapiro, *Death by a Thousand Cuts: The Fight over Taxing Inherited Wealth*, (Princeton: Princeton University Press, 2005).

[2] Non-business assets, such as cash, bonds, and publicly traded stock, are all relatively liquid assets. Under current estate tax rules, the basis of these assets is stepped up to the value at the time of death, thus eliminating the potential for capital gains taxes on inherited appreciation after liquidation.

[3] Some of the deferred tax is subject to a 2% interest payment. The provision allowing current use valuation requires a recapture tax, unless heirs continue to use the land in the business for at least 10 years. The market value can be reduced by a maximum of $750,000 through 1998. After 1998, the maximum is indexed for inflation, rounded to the next lowest multiple of $10,000. In 2004, the maximum was $850,000.

[4] The idea behind the minority discount is that heirs without control are constrained in the flow of income, and the possibility of sale. There are other related discounts, such as marketability discounts (because no ready market exists for the asset). There are concerns that these discounts are excessive in some cases and that they are used through estate planning to minimize estate taxes, and the Joint Tax Committee, in its study *Options to Improve Tax Compliance and Reform Tax Expenditures*, January 27, 2005, has proposed some revisions (see pp. 396-404).

[5] See CRS Report RS20593, *Asset Distribution of Taxable Estates: An Analysis*, by Steven Maguire.

[6] CRS Report RL30600, *Estate and Gift Taxes: Economic Issues*, by Donald J. Marples and Jane G. Gravelle.

[7] Congressional Budget Office, *Effects of the Federal Estate Tax on Farms and Small Businesses*, July 2005.

[8] Minority discounts ranged from an average of 16% for residential real estate to 51% for undeveloped land or farmland.

[9] The estate tax actually has graduated rates, but the exemption is effectively a credit, which means that the first dollar taxed is taxed at a rate in the middle of the tax schedule, rather than at the beginning as in the income tax. The first taxable dollar is effectively taxed at 41%, the rates rise to 55%, and there is also a 5% surcharge applying for estates between $10 million and $17.84 million to eliminate the advantages of the lower rate and exemption so that estates above this top limit are taxed at an average rate of 55%.

[10] Graetz and Shapiro, p. 36.

[11] This value is identified as the "cost-basis" of the asset. Ordinarily it is the original purchase price of the asset adjusted for improvements and depreciation in the case of physical assets.

[12] James M. Poterba and Scott Weisbenner, "The Distributional Burden of Taxing Estates and Unrealized Capital Gains at the Time of Death," National Bureau of Economic Research, Working Paper No. 7811, (Cambridge, MA: NBER, July 2000), p. 36.

[13] State estate and inheritance taxes vary by state. Many states have "decoupled" from the federal estate tax and levy stand alone estate and inheritance taxes.

[14] Neil E. Harl, "Taxation of Capital Gains, Gains at Death, and Estates: Policy Considerations," *Tax Notes, Special Report*, July 4, 2005, p. 10.

[15] This estimate is calculated by dividing $1.3 million by 35%.

[16] Reported in Joel Friedman and Ruth Carlitz, "Estate Tax Reform Could Raise Much-Needed Revenue," Center on Budget Policy and Priorities, March 16, 2005.

[17] See the Technical Appendix for the full development of the model.

[18] Also note, that if $d=t$, or the cap is set at the prevailing tax rate, the business exemption is simply the value of business assets less the regular exemption.

[19] Also note, that if $d=t$, or the cap is set at the prevailing tax rate, the business exemption is simply the value of business assets less the regular exemption.

In: Estate and Gift Taxes
Editor: Jacob A. Hughes

ISBN: 978-1-62100-516-2

Chapter 7

STATE ESTATE AND GIFT TAX REVENUE*

Steven Maguire

SUMMARY

P.L. 107-16, the Economic Growth and Tax Relief Reconciliation Act of 2001, repeals the federal estate tax for 2010 decedents. In addition, the act repealed the credit for state estate taxes for individuals dying after December 31, 2004, and replaced the credit with a deduction. In most states, the repeal of the tax and the significant increase in the federal exclusion will also repeal or diminish state estate, inheritance, and gift taxes. Some state budgets depend on the estate tax more than others. As a percentage of total tax revenue collected from FY2001 to FY2004, state estate tax contributions ranged from 0.19% in Alaska to 3.15% in Pennsylvania. After the federal credit for state estate taxes changed to a deduction in 2005, revenue collected from this tax source declined significantly, and in 2010, 29 states no longer levied estate or inheritance taxes. In the 111th Congress, H.R. 4154, passed by the House of Representatives on December 3, 2009, would permanently set the estate tax exemption level at $3.5 million per decedent, and proposals currently under consideration in the Senate would similarly retain the estate tax after repeal in 2010.

---

* This is an edited, reformatted and augmented version of a Congressional Research Service publication, CRS Report for Congress RS20853, from www.crs.gov, dated January 1, 2010.

INTRODUCTION

The federal estate tax has been repealed gradually by the Economic Growth and Tax Relief Reconciliation Act of 2001 (EGTRRA). Repeal of the federal estate tax and increase of the exclusion amount (or its credit equivalent) as prescribed by EGTRRA has also repealed or diminished most state estate, inheritance, and gift taxes.[1] In FY2001, state estate and gift tax revenue was 1.25% of total state tax revenue, but by FY2008 this proportion had decreased to 0.55% of total state tax revenue.[2] This report will briefly describe the federal credit for state estate taxes and provide data on the relative importance of estate, inheritance, and gift taxes to each state and the District of Columbia.

OVERVIEW

The federal credit for state estate taxes first appeared in the Revenue Act of 1924, some eight years after the introduction of the federal estate tax. The 1924 act stipulated that estates could claim a credit for state estate taxes up to 25% of the federal estate tax liability. After numerous modifications since its introduction, the federal credit was a schedule of 21 gradually increasing rates beginning at 0% and eventually reaching 16%. The rates were levied on the value of the net federal estate less a $60,000 exemption (the remainder was called the adjusted taxable estate). The top credit rate of 16% applied to adjusted taxable estate values over $10,040,000.

Changes under the Economic Growth and Tax Relief Reconciliation Act of 2001 (EGTRRA)

Because many state tax codes are linked directly to federal tax code, changes in federal law also affect the state tax codes. Two parts of EGTRRA affect the tax revenue generated by state estate taxes. First, EGTRRA phased out the federal credit for state death taxes for deaths occurring before January 1, 2005, and replaced it with a deduction beginning in 2005. The phase-out began in 2002 when the credit was reduced by 25%; by 50% in 2003; and by 75% in 2004. When estates began deducting state estate taxes, the value of the deduction (in terms of reduced tax liability) is the top marginal federal estate tax rate (45% in 2009) multiplied by state estate taxes paid. In contrast, before EGTRRA, the value of the credit was 100%, or it reduced federal tax liability dollar-for-dollar. Thus, after EGTRRA, state estate taxes impose a "real" tax liability or burden.

In addition, the applicable exclusion amount for federal estate taxes had increased to $3.5 million in 2009. The increase in the applicable exclusion amount is important to many states because it also serves as the filing threshold for the federal estate tax. Some states require estates to file a *state* return only when a federal return is required. If fewer federal estate tax returns are filed then fewer state estate tax returns would be filed.

States could avoid losing revenue by decoupling from the federal tax code, as some have since EGTRRA became law. However, the changes enacted by EGTRRA will necessarily create state estate tax burdens if states decouple from the federal tax code and collect estate tax revenue. If repeal of the federal estate tax is made permanent, the estates of those dying in states with a free standing estate tax would still pay state estate taxes. According to a recent examination of state estate tax laws conducted by the Center on Budget and Policy Priorities, 21 states and DC would have had a freestanding estate or inheritance tax in 2010 (see Table 1).[3] The next section provides data on state estate tax revenue as reported by the U.S. Census Bureau. The contribution of the estate tax to a state's finances likely influenced the decoupling decision. The more reliant states are less likely to repeal the tax.

STATE ESTATE AND GIFT TAX REVENUE

Before 2005, states imposed death-triggered taxes in one of two ways. Most states and the District of Columbia picked up the federal credit for state estate taxes as described above. Others collected an independent inheritance (or succession tax) and in most cases imposed an additional estate tax to absorb any remaining federal credit.

In states that previously picked up the federal credit, the state estate tax was repealed when the credit was repealed in 2005. In contrast, the states with an independent estate tax lost only the portion of their estate tax that relied on the existence of the federal credit.

For example, Pennsylvania maintains an inheritance tax which is applied with graduated rates and depends on the relationship of the heir to the decedent (lower rates for closer relatives), not the federal estate tax. Pennsylvania describes the inheritance tax on its official website:[4]

> Inheritance tax is imposed as a percentage of the value of a decedent's estate transferred to beneficiaries by will, heirs by intestacy and transferees by operation of law. The tax rate varies depending on the relationship of the heir to the decedent. Property owned jointly between husband and wife is exempt from inheritance tax. Inheritance tax payments are due upon the death of the decedent and become delinquent nine months after the individual's death. If inheritance tax is paid within three months of the decedent's death, a 5 percent discount is allowed.

The 21 states that collect an estate or inheritance tax in 2010 are identified in Table 1 with a "yes" in the final column. Twelve of these states, and the Distict of Columbia, have estate taxes that are similar to the pick-up taxes levied before 2005. Nine states have standalone estate or inheritance taxes, while two states, Maryland and New Jersey, levy both an estate tax previously tied to the federal tax, as well as a separate inheritance tax.

In addition to providing information about the existence of the state estate tax in 2010, Table 1 also presents data on the relative importance of estate and gift taxes to each state using the average tax revenue generated by state estate taxes for FY2001 to FY2004, and FY2005 to FY2008. The average annual revenue over these two four-year intervals is provided because state estate tax revenue fluctuates significantly from year to year. In particular, these two time periods were chosen because they represent the first four years before and after the state estate credit was repealed under EGTRRA. To facilitate comparison across these two intervals, annual tax revenue data have been adjusted for inflation.

Along with year-to-year fluctuations within states, there is considerable variation among the states in proportion of the total state tax revenue accounted for by the estate tax. For FY2001 to FY2004, Alaska's estate tax amounted to only 0.19% of tax revenues, and 0.03% for FY2005 to FY2008. On the otherhand, Pennsylvania's inheritance tax comprised 3.15% of the state's total tax revenues for FY2001 to FY2004, and 2.48% of tax revenue for FY2005 to FY2008.

Further, there is also significant variation within states across time. New Hampshire collected 2.69% of its total tax revenue from the estate tax during FY2001 to FY2004, but only 0.19% of total tax revenue from FY2005 to FY2008. Similarly, the estate tax comprised 2.39% of total tax revenue for South Dakota during FY2001 to FY2004, but only 0.13% of tax revenue from FY2005 to FY2008.

Table 1. State Estate and Gift Tax Revenue: 2001 to 2004 and 2005 to 2008

	Revenue from Estate and Gift Tax Average (in $000s)[a]		Estate and Gift Taxes as % of Total Tax Revenue Average		Reliance on Estate and Gift Taxes Rank		Estate or Inheritance Tax
State	2001-2004	2005-2008	2001-2004	2005-2008	2001-2004	2005-2008	2010
Alabama	57,399	4,658	0.71%	0.05%	39	46	no
Alaska	2,747	612	0.19%	0.03%	51	51	no
Arizona	88,266	12,243	0.86%	0.10%	31	34	no
Arkansas	43,300	4,416	0.71%	0.06%	38	44	no
California	1,019,773	62,948	1.04%	0.06%	21	45	no
Colorado	76,939	8,374	0.92%	0.10%	27	36	no
Connecticut	221,205	213,205	1.93%	1.63%	6	4	yes
Delaware	39,591	3,129	1.54%	0.95%	9	13	yes
Dist. of Columbia[b]	69,489	45,311	1.81%	0.10%	7	33	yes
Florida	712,561	114,630	2.30%	0.30%	5	26	no
Georgia	120,220	15,056	0.72%	0.09%	37	41	no
Hawaii	17,647	4,659	0.42%	0.09%	49	37	no
Idaho	22,675	2,971	0.76%	0.09%	35	39	no
Illinois	340,492	316,386	1.24%	1.04%	14	12	yes

Table 1. (Continued).

State	Revenue from Estate and Gift Tax Average (in $000s)[a]		Estate and Gift Taxes as % of Total Tax Revenue Average		Reliance on Estate and Gift Taxes Rank		Estate or Inheritance Tax
	2001-2004	2005-2008	2001-2004	2005-2008	2001-2004	2005-2008	2010
Indiana	190,255	159,841	1.50%	1.10%	11	11	yes
Iowa	91,105	80,479	1.51%	1.22%	10	8	yes
Kansas	54,337	53,618	0.92%	0.79%	26	19	no
Kentucky	99,293	53,753	1.03%	0.53%	22	23	yes
Louisiana	76,180	17,045	0.86%	0.17%	30	28	no
Maine	34,380	53,207	1.07%	1.44%	19	6	yes
Maryland	190,926	228,790	1.45%	1.48%	12	5	yes
Massachusetts	230,331	251,006	1.22%	1.20%	16	9	yes
Michigan	136,814	28,368	0.51%	0.11%	45	32	no
Minnesota	98,206	132,655	0.61%	0.72%	42	22	yes
Mississippi	28,359	4,112	0.49%	0.07%	47	43	no
Missouri	129,674	15,552	1.24%	0.15%	15	29	no
Montana	17,449	1,829	0.98%	0.09%	24	40	no
Nebraska	24,996	31,146	0.65%	0.74%	41	21	yes
Nevada	39,026	7,564	0.81%	0.13%	34	30	no

State	Revenue from Estate and Gift Tax Average (in $000s)[a]		Estate and Gift Taxes as % of Total Tax Revenue Average		Reliance on Estate and Gift Taxes Rank		Estate or Inheritance Tax
	2001-2004	2005-2008	2001-2004	2005-2008	2001-2004	2005-2008	2010
New Hampshire	59,981	4,193	2.69%	0.19%	2	27	no
New Jersey	575,298	633,572	2.49%	2.26%	3	2	yes
New Mexico	23,255	2,205	0.52%	0.04%	44	49	no
New York	877,062	1,009,235	1.70%	1.65%	8	3	yes
North Carolina	158,842	172,611	0.85%	0.78%	32	20	yes
North Dakota	6,091	863	0.44%	0.05%	48	47	no
Ohio	133,034	126,496	0.55%	0.48%	43	24	yes
Oklahoma	105,087	74,210	1.44%	0.89%	13	14	no
Oregon	68,315	87,571	1.02%	1.15%	23	10	yes
Pennsylvania	862,986	776,913	3.15%	2.48%	1	1	yes
Rhode Island	29,107	37,556	1.09%	1.31%	17	7	yes
South Carolina	56,217	6,629	0.76%	0.08%	36	42	no
South Dakota	28,260	1,579	2.39%	0.13%	4	31	no
Tennessee	107,997	97,802	1.08%	0.85%	18	17	yes
Texas	315,511	34,177	0.91%	0.09%	28	38	no
Utah	24,346	2,958	0.51%	0.05%	46	48	no
Vermont	16,776	20,745	0.89%	0.81%	29	18	yes

Table 1. (Continued).

State	Revenue from Estate and Gift Tax Average (in $000s)[a]		Estate and Gift Taxes as % of Total Tax Revenue Average		Reliance on Estate and Gift Taxes Rank		Estate or Inheritance Tax
	2001-2004	2005-2008	2001-2004	2005-2008	2001-2004	2005-2008	2010
Virginia	163,109	162,185	1.04%	0.88%	20	15	no
Washington	142,706	80,075	0.93%	0.44%	25	25	yes
West Virginia	15,137	1,543	0.36%	0.03%	50	50	no
Wisconsin	92,890	131,089	0.65%	0.88%	40	16	no
Wyoming	11,463	2,023	0.81%	0.10%	33	35	no
United States	159,747	105,761	1.10%	0.59%	n/a	n/a	n/a

Sources: U.S. Bureau of Census, State Government Tax Collections: 2001-2008; Elizabeth C. McNichol, "State Taxes on Inherited Wealth Remain Common: 23 States Levy an Estate or Inheritance Tax," *Center on Budget and Policy Priorities*, December 16, 2009; and author's calculations.

[a] To adjust for inflation, the consumer price index was used to convert all estate and gift tax annual revenue estimates for 2001-2007 into 2008 dollars.

[b] The District of Columbia tax data were collected from its FY2005 proposed budget, and from revenue estimates for FY2004-FY2008.

Table 1 also reports the relative rank of states based upon their reliance on state estate and gift taxes over FY2001 to FY2004 and FY2005 to FY2008. States such as New Jersey and Pennslyvania relied significantly on estate or inheritance taxes during both four-year intervals, while Alaska and West Virgina depended relatively little on estate taxes during these time periods. Florida, New Hampshire, and South Dakota ranked highly in terms of reliance on estate and gift taxes from FY2001 to FY2004, but received considerably lower rankings during FY2005 to FY2008.

ACKNOWLEDGMENTS

This report was updated with the assistance of Andrew Hanna.

End Notes

[1] For the remainder of the report, all state taxes that are triggered by death will be referred to as "state estate taxes." "State estate taxes," thus include state inheritance taxes, succession taxes, and estate taxes. Additionaly, unless otherwise noted, tax data from the District of Columbia are included in the aggregated state estate tax revenue totals discussed in this report.

[2] U.S. Census Bureau, Governments Division, *State Government Tax Collections*, website http://www.census.gov/govs/www/statetax05.html, visited December 24, 2009. All state estate tax revenue figures presented in this report have been adjusted for inflation using the consumer price index, with 2008 as the baseline year (e.g., all revenue totals have been converted to 2008 dollars).

[3] Elizabeth C. McNichol, "State Taxes on Inherited Wealth Remain Common: 23 States Levy an Estate or Inheritance Tax," *Center on Budget and Policy Priorities*, December 16, 2009.

[4] The site is http://www.portal.state.pa.us/portal/server.pt/community/inheritance_tax/11414, visited December 29, 2009.

INDEX

F

G

H

I